Helen K. Ingram

Tourists' and Settlers' Guide to Florida

Helen K. Ingram

Tourists' and Settlers' Guide to Florida

ISBN/EAN: 9783337193621

Printed in Europe, USA, Canada, Australia, Japan

Cover: Foto ©Lupo / pixelio.de

More available books at **www.hansebooks.com**

THE GREAT HOTELS

OF THE

EAST COAST

AT

St. Augustine, Ormond and

Palm Beach,

AND THE

Famous Orange Groves,

Pineapple Plantations, etc., of the Country Tributary to

INDIAN RIVER, LAKE WORTH
And BISCAYNE BAY,

Are reached only via the

Florida East Coast Railway.

JOSEPH RICHARDSON,
General Passenger Agent,
St. Augustine.

TOURISTS'
· AND ·
SETTLERS' GUIDE

TO FLORIDA

· BY ·

H. K. INGRAM

JACKSONVILLE, FLORIDA.

1895-6.

It is Florida.

...

Knowest thou the land where the lemon
    trees bloom,
  Where the gold orange glows in the green
    thicket's gloom ;
Where the winds ever soft from the blue
    heavens blow,
  Where the stately magnolia and dark myrtle
    grow ;
Where beams the fair sun, where the mock-
    ing birds sing,
  And all the year offers the blessings of spring.

PREFACE.

No pretense is made that a "Guide to Florida" is a new or novel publication. There have been guides almost beyond number, guides issued by land companies and other corporations, which guided the traveler to certain sections and ignored all other portions of the State. Most commendable enterprise without doubt when viewed from the company's point of view, but worthless to the invalid or tourist who sought health or recreation in the ONE Florida.

From the tourists' and settlers' stand-point no thorough, reliable work of the kind has ever been issued. There has ever existed a distinct want of such a publication, and this book is offered to supply this need.

It is not designed to furnish rapturous descriptions of Florida, appropriate as they always are, and great as is the temptation whenever the subject is broached. The man who contemplates either visiting the State or becoming an inhabitant thereof, it is hoped will find his natural questions either answered beforehand, or himself guided to the proper parties for obtaining correct information. Facts and figures, dollars and cents, will abound. Expense of travel, cost of living, and all practical questions are anticipated and answered.

The book will be issued annually hereafter, and it may safely be promised will become more and more valuable to both the traveler and the business man as the years go by.

The fact that the author has often visited every portion of the State and repeatedly written up each section, and has her knowledge from personal observation and close inquiry, will, it is hoped, add value and interest to the book. Moreover, it is Florida up-to-date containing the latest statistics and situations.

The Hotel and Boarding House directory is perfectly reliable. The tourist may easily estimate his expenses by consulting the transportation tables and the directory.

A limited number of advertisements, such as Real Estate Agencies, Liveries, Druggists, etc., which are of real value to the settler, investor, invalid and pleasure seeker, have been admitted.

While many guide books are overloaded with all sorts of advertisements, the nice discrimination which will be practiced in the getting up of this book will be such that its great value will be its advertisements.

HOW TO REACH FLORIDA.

BY RAIL.

The shortest and most direct line from New York and the Atlantic cities is by the new Florida Short Line of the Southern Railway and Florida Central and Peninsular Railroad. This deviates but little from a straight line from New York to Tampa. The trip from New York to Jacksonville is accomplished in 28 hours. The route is often called the "Piedmont Air Line" because it skirts the foot of the Appalachian mountains and winds through unsurpassed scenery and much of the way through country every mile of which is historical. Fare from New York to Jacksonville $29.15; from Philadelphia $26.65; from Washington $22.65.

The Plant System.

By its connections with the Pennsylvania R. R. and Atlantic Coast Line to Charleston, also makes a direct trip from New York to Tampa, where by close connection with its steamships the trip is continued without interruption to Key West, Cuba, and Jamaica. Fare from New York via Washington, Richmond, Weldon, Raleigh, Wilmington, Charleston, Savannah, Waycross to Jacksonville $29.15; from Philadelphia $26.65; from Washington $22.65.

The Jacksonville, Tampa and Key West Railway.

Has its connections to New York and the East by all the routes, but begins properly at Jacksonville and permeates all the central, eastern and western portions of the State.

The East Coast and Keys.

In the same way begins properly at Jacksonville, and is the only direct line to the East Coast, the wonderful

Indian River country and the newly discovered marvels of Lake Worth and Biscayne Bay.

The Florida Central and Peninsular Railroad.

By its connections with the Louisville & Nashville and Pacific & Atlantic affords entrance at the extreme western portion of the State at Pensacola and Flomaton, from all points west and southwest. Also, by its connection with the Southern Railway from western and northwestern points, entrance is afforded Florida at Everett, and thence to points east and south. By its association with the Southern Railway it offers, as above stated, the shortest line to New York and other Eastern cities. The Plant System, in like manner, leads in from the west at Live Oak, thence east, or down the west coast direct. Fare from Denver $42.65; from Detroit $28.20; from Chicago $25.00; from Cincinnati $20.90.

BY WATER.

The principal line of steamers from New York is the Clyde Line. This line keeps five large and elegantly appointed steamers continually on the route between Jacksonville and New York. They are the "Seminole," "Iroquois," "Cherokee," "Yemassee" and "Algonquin." One of these steamers leaves New York from Pier 29, East River, at 3 p. m., every Monday, Wednesday and Friday.

One of them leaves Jacksonville from the Clyde Dock, foot of Hogan street, every Sunday, Tuesday and Thursday. All call at Charleston, S. C., both ways.

Fare, one way, $25.00; round trip, $43.30.

This company has also two fast freight steamers, the "Delaware" and "Winyah," which sail from Jacksonville to Philadelphia direct, but call at Charleston, S. C., when south bound.

TRAVEL VIA

J. T. & K. W.

RAILWAY
IN FLORIDA.

A North and South Line Thro' the

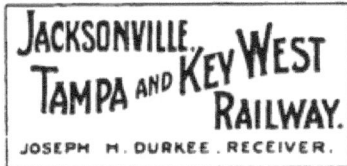

Heart of Florida.

For Details Try It.

or address any authorized representative.

Through Coaches and Pullman Sleepers.

W. B. COFFIN,　　　　　　　　　G. D. ACKERLY,
　Gen'l Sup't.　　　　　　　　　　Gen'l Pass. Agt.

Jacksonville, Florida.

THE SHORT LINE
BETWEEN
FLORIDA AND THE NORTH.

THE
Florida Central and Peninsular
RAILROAD.

Double Daily Trains
BETWEEN
NEW YORK AND JACKSONVILLE,
Connecting also with St. Augustine.

These trains run via Savannah, Columbia, Lynchburg, Washington, Baltimore and Philadelphia, connecting over same line for *ASHEVILLE*, and the favorite resorts of the Mountains of Virginia and the Carolinas.

Double Daily Trains
BETWEEN
MACON, ATLANTA AND JACKSONVILLE.
In connection with the Southern Railway—the only line *entering the* *EXPOSITION GROUNDS.*

Daily Between Cincinnati and Jacksonville.
The Cincinnati and Florida Limited, a vestibuled train, making close connection with Chicago, Detroit, Cleveland, Louisville, and all points West.

Daily between St. Louis, Kansas City, Chicago, all Arkansas and Missouri points, and Jacksonville.

Only line between **NEW ORLEANS** and **JACKSONVILLE** with through Sleepers. Runs through the beautiful Middle Florida Hill Country—Pensacola and Escambia Bay.

All these trains connect with St. Augustine, the Indian River and St. Johns River points, direct for Ocala, Gainesville, Leesburg, Orlando, Winter Park, and all West Coast points. **Hunting and Fishing Resorts.** Send for list. Send for best Indexed Map of Florida.

NORTHERN AGENCIES:
J. L. Adams, General Eastern Agent, 353 Broadway, New York.
W. B. Pennington, General Western Agent, 169 Walnut street, Cincinnati.
E. D. Palmer, Agent, 197 Washington street, Boston.
Daniel Lammot, Southern Agent, 50 S. Third street, Philadelphia.
John R. Duval, Agent, 205 E. Baltimore street, Baltimore.
H. F. Davis, Commercial Building, St. Louis.
G. W. Carhart, Endicott Building, St. Paul, Minn.

N. S. PENNINGTON, Traffic Manager.
WALTER G. COLEMAN, A. O. MacDONELL,
Gen. Trav. Agt., Jacksonville, Fla. Gen. Pass. Agt., Jacksonville, Fla.

The Mallory Steamship Line.

The Mallory Steamship Line sails to New York and Boston, stopping at Philadelphia *en route*. Passengers from Jacksonville take the steamer train every Thursday at 7:30 a. m. on the Florida Central and Peninsular Railway at the Union Depot, and are carried to Fernandina. Here they are met by the Cumberland boat, which conveys them by the inland route to Brunswick, Ga., where they take the ocean steamer. Fare from Jacksonville to New York, first-class, $22.50; intermediate, $17.50; steerage, $12.50; round trip, $40.30.

The Ocean Steamship Company.

This company, known as the Savannah Line, carries passengers by rail from Jacksonville to Savannah, where they take the steamer for New York every Tuesday, Friday and Sunday. This line also runs a steamer from Savannah to Boston every Thursday.

Fare, $25.00 for first-class, one way; $19.00 for intermediate, one way, or $43.30 for round trip.

The Merchants' and Miners' Transportation Company.

The Merchants' and Miners' Transportation Company's steamers sail between Savannah and Baltimore. Passengers are conveyed to and from Jacksonville to Savannah by rail. The steamers leave Savannah, north-bound, every Wednesday and Saturday. Fare between Baltimore and Jacksonville, $20.65; round trip, $36.30.

The Clyde Line has, in winter, a St. Johns River service, when the two steamers, "Fred'k de Bary" and "City of Jacksonville" ply between Jacksonville and Sanford and all intervening points. Besides these, the "John Sylvester," one of the finest steamers on Florida waters, makes the same run. Smaller steamers, such as the "May Garner," make the run to Green Cove Springs and Palatka.

Southern Railway,

The Greatest Southern System.

Short Line
BETWEEN

Florida and the East

Via Savannah,
Columbia,
Charlotte,
and Washington,

Short Line to the North and West via Atlanta

ONLY LINE
To the Land of the Sky.

Superior Through Car Service.
Schedules Unequaled.

W. D. ALLEN, F. P. A., Jacksonville, Fla.
W. A. TURK, G. P. A.,   S. H. HARDWICK, A. G. P. A.,
Washington, D. C.   Atlanta, Ga.

"The Three Brothers" will run this winter from Jacksonville to Nassau, N. P., in the Bahamas.

FLORIDA

The Name.

THE origin of this much discussed name is still an open queston of the writers on this subject, many of whom insist that the land was first seen on Palm Sunday, or, as they erroneously say, "*Pascua Florida.*" The Spanish name for Palm Sunday is "*Domingo de ramos.*" The Hebrew term for the Passover is "*Pascha*" from whence we have the French "*Pasque*" and the Spanish "*Pascua,*" which the Saxon called Easter. In a book printed in London in 1763 is the following quaint passage: "It hath been already observed that this country (Florida) was first discovered in 1497 by John Cabot, a Venetian mariner in the service of Henry VII, King of England. It was more *completely discovered* in the year 1512 by Juan Ponce de Leon, a Spaniard, who gave it the name of Florida because it was seen first in Easter, called *Pasqua de flores* in the language of his country, or as Herreva alledges, because it was covered with flowers, and the most beautiful blossoms"

Those who have seen the Easter season in Florida and the wealth of flowers which still commemorate and adorn its return, can well believe that both these reasons influenced the giving of its name. And as Easter Sunday revealed it to his view, behold the land was decked with flowers and the river freighted with the pure white lilies which were associated with the feast from days of old. No marvel that he exclaimed "Pascua de flores"—an Easter of flowers. Quoting again from the same authority, we find this grave assertion :

"The air is pure and temperate and the country generally speaking exceedingly salubrious. Hence it is that the natives of Florida are supposed to derive that strength and robustness of constitution which distinguishes them from the more southern Indians. The soil is rich and fertile, producing in great abundance all kinds of timber and fruit trees. There is no species of vegetable but may be raised with little trouble in Florida. As to cotton, it is so plentiful that most of the civilized inhabitants are clothed of a manufacture composed of that useful natural production." This author then describes the flax, hemp, pearls, rubies, and gold; the iron and coal, the "amber grease," and tar, the corn, pulse, roots and herbs, fruits and sassafras, the cassava and indigo, the grapes and prunes, the beef, veal and mutton, and states that horses were to be had for the value of a crown in European commodities. Then is described the settlement of St. Augustine, on the day devoted to that saint in 1565, its capture by Sir Francis Drake in 1586; its destruction in 1665, and the final cession of Florida to England, which, as the author observes, was "an acquisition of the utmost importance to our cotton manufactures." Again he says:

"According to all accounts, the *Floridians* were in *North America* what the *Athenians* were in *Greece*; and it is to be regretted that the original manners of them, and many other people in *South America* are now lost by the infection they have received from the *Spaniards* and the *Europeans*."

It is interesting to know that the climate and salubrity, fertility and productions of Florida were thus justly estimated and understood at such an early date; and indeed, to these descriptions but little can now be added save in detail, and nothing needs to be changed, for the gold and precious stones which they found in the "Apalachian mountains" and the coal and iron of Alabama and Georgia,

A Winter Scene in Florida.

which States then were within the boundaries of Florida, are enriching the country today.

Of the further history of Florida a volume of intense interest could be written, but as the past is ever but a dream and the future but a hope, yet in this case a sure and certain hope, it is the ever-living present, the bustling progressive present, the beautiful and joyous present, which commands a more lively attention.

The Second Discovery of Florida,

May be said to have been made by the Federal troops during the Civil War. When they invaded the land, and found flowers blooming in the open air in January, century plants sending up flowering stalks 40 feet in height, and discovered that they could themselves plunge into the St. John's for a swimming contest in February, their rapturous accounts attracted attention. Their officers, who had never before seen a winter without ice, snow and frost could scarcely believe their own senses, and many of them, in after years, remembering its delights, came to its shores to seek permanent homes.

While it is the oldest of the States, it is, at the same time a comparatively new State—not yet developed, indeed, not fully explored, but attracting for the past twenty years or more, the best class of citizens from all the older parts of the Union. The cultivation of the orange and other fruits which, under the old regime, was limited to door yard ornaments and home consumption, under the new impulse, became established industries, and with their successful growth the fame of the State received a new accession. The discovery within the past few years of valuable minerals beneath her unpromising looking sands, has completed the conquest of capital and enterprise which her climate and products had begun.

Climate.

The climate is a continuous marvel, for here two zones

vie with each other, giving their best to this border land between them. The difference in the monthly mean temperature the year around is seldom more than 30°. Surgeon General Lawson, of the United States Army, says in his official report about Florida:

"As respects *health*, the climate of Florida stands preeminent. That the peninsular climate of Florida is much more salubrious than that of any other State in the Union is clearly established by the medical statistics of the army. Indeed, the statistics in this bureau demonstrate the fact that the diseases which result from malaria are of a much milder type in the peninsula of Florida than in any other State in the Union. These records show that the ratio of deaths to the number of cases of remittent fever has been much less than among the troops serving in any other portion of the United States. In the middle division of the United States the proportion is one death to thirty-six cases of remittent fever; in the Northern division one to fifty-two; in the Southern division one to fifty-four, in Texas, one to seventy-eight; in California, one to one hundred and forty-eight; while in Florida it is but *one to two hundred and eighty-seven*. In short, it may be asserted, without fear of refutation, that Florida possesses a much more agreeable and salubrious climate than any other State or Territory in the Union."

Possibly one secret of the fascinations which Florida wields over all who tarry long in her border, is the great variety of her productions. Omitting an enumeration of the brilliant sisterhood of flowers that border her lakes, almost choke her rivers, and gleam in her bosky dells and shady swamps, we give a brief mention of those products which offer to her settlers, home-seekers, and established residents, the means of winning bread and butter, and surrounding themselves and their families with all the comforts of life.

The mere mention of the word Florida, suggests the other word

Oranges.

Now is approached a subject which about 69 millions of people in the United States believe to be a dead issue.

It is well that the right shall prevail and the truth be known. The world of late years has heard never a word of Florida unless associated with orange groves, and for a few months past of nothing but frost and dead trees and destroyed prosperity.

Now the fact is that people who live in Florida a number of years grow very peculiar in one or two particulars. The first is, that they are so accustomed to a state of health that when they hear of the many epidemics of diptheria and scarlet fever and pneumonia, and summer complaint, and meningitis which in many northern sections are annual visitants, they scarcely comprehend the dire calamities. Another is that Floridians by adoption or otherwise are only habituated to nature in its Florida aspect, and when a little of the cold from the Western plains escapes or flows over upon them by mistake, or through malice and envy, they are absolutely dismayed. Now if they were accustomed to have wheat and oats and spring crops frozen down nearly every year, or washed away by flood or drowned out by superfluous rainfall, or their peach orchards frozen down every year or two, or all the peach crop frequently destroyed as it is in New Jersey and Delaware, or rivers flowing through the streets and into the cellars every spring, while the inhabitants move out for a few days to contemplate the watery waste, or were familiar with the Kansas potato bug or the numerous western grasshoppers and other things which are every day matters in the north and west they would have not been so astonished as they were by last winter's cold snaps. As a matter of fact many orange growers planted other crops at once after the freeze and have made more profits than they would have realized from their oranges. As the soil in the groves was well fertilized and cultivated the change of crop was advantageous to its productiveness. To the joy of the owner the orange trees also began to grow from the root, and from every part of the State the reports come that the groves are doing well. Next year when the fruit comes into market, Florida oranges will show up *very much alive* and the tourist will see what a mistake he has made not to buy a grove while the depression lasted. The State has not, of course, recovered from the blow to its prosperity, but the state of mind has changed, and every one is assured that it is not a greater misfortune than sometimes happens anywhere and everywhere.

Pineapples.

So wide spreading and severe was the freeze of Feb. '95, that the pineapples in the extreme southern portions of the State, were frozen so that the fruitage of '95 did not appear. Only those groves under so-called shelters, or open lattice work were spared. But so recuperative and forceful is this wonderful climate, that now, in the early autumn and winter of '95, a traveler riding along the southeastern portion of the peninsula passes through eighteen miles of an almost unbroken stretch of pineapple fields which will all afford fruitage in May and June of '96. Immense fields of the spiny plants stretch away on either side of the track as far as the eye can reach, seeming like the great corn fields of the west or the cotton plantations of the south. They have all been set out since the freeze of February last, but as they take but two years to perfect fruit, the world need not long be deprived of this luxury.

Tobacco.

About the year 1565, Sir John Hawkins carried tobacco to England, and it is interesting to note what an important factor tobacco has been in the commerce of the world. Though an article of luxury, it was in the early history of Florida looked upon as a convenient medium of exchange. In 1620, while there was an abundance of tobacco in the colonies, there was a great scarcity of females.

An enterprising trader brought ninety young women from England to America and exchanged to the planter 120 weight of female for 150 pounds of tobacco. King James issued a proclamation restricting this unlawful and obnoxious traffic. In 1570 Florida tobacco was first taken to Holland, and not until 1616 did the colonists of Virginia begin the planting of tobacco, the seed being obtained from what was then known as the Spanish Possessions—Florida.

Florida tobacco was a favorite article with an extensive foreign and domestic trade many years ago—in *ante bellum* times. What was grown then commanded a high price, frequently as much as a dollar a pound. But at the close of the war, shifting labor and the alluring price of cotton, caused a decline of the industry in those sections where it had most flourished. About six years ago experiments began to be made in the State, and the results have been magical. All tests gave favorable indications; experts were delighted; manufacturers became interested; capital was enlisted, and now there is a clamor for Florida tobacco; the industry is again taking on considerable proportions and bids fair, in a short time, to outstrip any other in the State, and to carry the country by storm with its aromatic product.

Those of our farmers who have followed up this industry have gained an experience in the cultivation and handling of tobacco, which yields them a constantly increasing profit. Eight to nine months in the year are afforded for the growing and housing of the different crops—and two at least should be cut from the same planting; worms are not so troublesome as in other sections; there is no danger of injury from hail or frost; expensive barns are not required for curing; no heating, or drying, or moistening apparatus, the climate being peculiarly favorable to perfect curing by natural process, as also to handling and manipulating throughout—from the field to the factory. Florida tobacco is now largely used in some of the first factories of New York to take the place of the more expensive Sumatran and Cuban articles, to the latter of which it is equal in quality both as filler and wrapper, and to the former as wrapper alone—facts repeatedly proven, and everywhere acknowledged and sustained, and the demand now far outstrips the supply. The climate of Florida is so favorable to the cultivation of tobacco, that, aside from the first or original crop, two sucker crops can be raised. This is accomplished by cutting the stock off near the ground and leaving a sucker or shoot on the root, which will in a short time grow into a healthy, well developed stock, on which the leaves will be lighter in weight, but larger and finer than the first crop. This, we believe, is an advantage enjoyed in no other tobacco-producing State in this country, as late springs and early frosts in the fall render a second or third crop in other sections an impossibility.

Florida's total production of tobacco last season was over a million pounds, on less than two thousand acres; value of crop to producers, $300,000.

To the tobacco growers of Florida, the present disturbed conditions in Cuba, means a harvest of shekels. The war-cloud has intercepted both the growth and the shipment of tobacco from the Queen of the Antilles. The tobacco growers of Gadsden county in this State are surprised by offers of 35 cents per pound for tobacco that formerly brought but 12½ to 15 cents per pound. Mr. Saxon of Tallahassee began this year the experiment of raising chewing tobacco, and his elated manner and smiling face as he gets his returns from shipments prove that he chose the golden moment in which to try his luck.

Timber.

Here also meet and intermingle the products of two zones. The hickory, pine, cedar and maple of the far north grow in loving brotherhood beside the stately and magnificent magnolia, the tropical palmetto and the fragrant myrtle; while the holly decks itself with its red berries near to the white-beaded mystic mistletoe. Two hundred varieties of timber (more than any other State can offer) invite the manufacturer. Herds of cattle roaming at will and feeding the year around on the wild cane and luxuriant grasses of the wide savannas of its south-central portion; the thick-skinned manatee and the tough-skinned alligator, with the palmetto, richer in tannic acid than any other substance, everywhere in superabundance, offer a combination of inducements to the manufacturer of leather which no other land can equal.

Sugar.

As a sugar producer Florida ranks first. Her climate enables the planter to gather his crop for from seven to fifteen years without replanting, and thus she ranks with Cuba and the Sandwich Islands.

In the southern portion of the State an extensive drainage system has lowered the water in the great lakes from 10 to 20 feet. This has rendered useful millions of acres upon which sugar cane will return the first year in green cane the whole cost of the land, planting and cultivation. If the planter also refines his product the profit will be marvelously increased. The next year the crop will be almost entirely profit, no replanting being necessary, and the cultivation being less than $10.00 per acre. This is an unfailing crop and the season of gathering lasts nearly all winter with no risk of frost which is the bane of the Louisiana planter, and every year comes too soon for his interests.

This valuable crop is universally grown by the farmers throughout the State, and its products are staple luxuries on their tables and in the local markets the year round, while a good deal is also exported. New Florida syrup has no competitor, and nothing to compare with it aside from the new crop maple, to which it is fully equal in the estimation of many. No other crop enters so fully into the domestic and social life of the planter. Our "canegrindings" and "sugar-boilings" in the late fall and early winter are favorite evening gatherings for the young, of town and country, very like the New England "maple-parties." They make a not unpleasant picture about the kettles and furnaces at night. Cane needs a rich, and prefers a moist soil, but will grow on any but the poorest and driest. The yield is largely increased by liberally fertilizing, or by "cow penning" the ground beforehand, when it will produce on any of our better grade pine lands as well as the hammocks. According to soil and season, the yield may be as low as eight or ten, or run as high as eighteen or twenty barrels of syrup per acre. The general average may be placed at from twelve to fifteen. The yield in crude sugar would be about two hundred pounds to the barrel, worth about five cents per pound in the local market; the syrup, forty to fifty cents per gallon—about thirty-five gallons to the barrel. The profit per acre, one year with another, may safely be put down at $100 and upwards. The "green" and "ribbon" canes are mostly grown. A great deal is sold in the stalk and consumed in the local markets, and at home, for "chewing," and it is surprising how much disappears in this way. This offers a most profitable manner of disposal to the grower, as it brings from two and a half to five cents a stalk.

This is one of our "coming industries," and Florida is destined to be a great sugar-producing State.

Rice.

Rice is a profitable crop, and considerable is produced, equal in quality to the best, and mostly exported. It is generally grown upon land too wet for anything else, but upland rice is as easily produced. It is planted from March to June, and harvested from late summer to early fall. Two crops are sometimes taken from the same stubbles. The average yield is from twenty to sixty bushels, and has been known to reach 200 per acre. It is worth from 75 cents to

$1.25 per bushel in the rough. Stock of all kinds relish the straw.

Cotton.

Florida's claim to distinction as a cotton State is founded on her production of sea-island, or long staple, black seeded cotton. Florida produces one-third of all this staple grown in the United States, and one-sixth of the world's supply, Egypt alone appearing in the light of a rival. Florida cotton is the standard for the article in the great markets of the world. It grows on all Florida lands, and the yield is greatly increased by properly fertilizing. The average yield without this is from 300 to 500 pounds of seed cotton per acre, though some planters obtain as much as 600 to 1,000, with its use. It yields a pound of lint, or ginned cotton, to about three and a half of the seed.

The other products are cotton seed meal, cake and oil, the former a splendid fertilizer (as are also the hulls and ashes) and stock and cattle food. The oil is now a staple article in the markets and industries of the world, appearing under the guise of lard, olive oil, etc., for cooking, table use, and the canning of sardines. The seed is worth $12.50 per ton, and yields in products more than twice that amount. the stalks are said to yield a fibre almost equal to jute. The upland, or short staple, though produced easily and abundantly here, is almost entirely neglected for the superior article.

Of the sea-island cotton, almost the entire output is handled by the firm of H. F. Dutton & Co., of Gainesville, Fla., Providence. R. I., and Alexandria, Egypt.

The great Paisley firm of Scotland uses Florida sea-island cotton exclusively for the manufacture of the celebrated Coates' spool thread. Mr. John L. Inglis, of Madison, is their principal inspector, selector and buyer.

The equally well known Clarke firm of Lanark, Scotland, manufacturers of the O. N. T. spool cotton, procure all their supplies from Florida.

Phosphate.

Phosphate is in vegetable growth especially of fruit and food-producing plants one of the most easily exhausted elements of the soil and is but second in importance. For many years the farmer of the United States has been educated to believe that he must get from South America the guano which his farm needs, and when he hears that Nature has bestowed this necessary element in great abundance within the limits of his own country, the fact is too wonderful to be immediately accepted. Its discovery marks an epoch in the history of geological science in America, as it reverses theories, and what was regarded as geologically young, it demonstrates to be really geologically old. Since Florida contains the oldest city in the sisterhood of States, it is but poetic justice and singularly appropriate that it should also have a more ancient foundation. This formation lies so near the surface in Florida that it is easily mined and the cost of placing it upon the market is less that in any other known region. Spain and Canada have ores of richer grade but impassable mountains guard the one, and an inhospitable climate the other. These countries for these reasons cannot compete in the markets of the world with Florida's phosphate. The story of its discovery is like that of many other valuable gifts of the earth to man, almost an accident. Yet when man becomes conscious of a need Nature seems ever ready at the auspicious moment to reveal to him her treasures for his use, and to teach him to bind new powers to his service when his advancement demands. At the present time Florida nearly equals the output of South Carolina whose mines have been famous for over a century.

As to the profit of the industry it is sufficient to state that it is more than double the percentages realized in South Carolina, which have long enriched alike the State and the private investors. This is owing to the natural conditions which render the cost so much less to the Florida miner while the material is from 10 to 20 per cent superior in quality.

Other minerals of economic value which are also found in quantity are kaolin, pure ochres of several shades from orange yellow to brilliant red, native cement and moss agate, potash and chloride of silver and Fuller's earth. Florida abounds in mineral springs and many of them contain iron, so it is among the possibilities that iron is also here.

Florida at Atlanta.

Florida is to be well represented at the Atlanta Exposition. For her great antiquity, the bones of the mammoth and tiger side by side will testify. Manatees and tarpon will illustrate the wondrous life of her waters. Phosphate, both rock and pebble, will be there in quantity and, with kaolin, will demonstrate her wealth of minerals, which no gold mines can rival in value. Corn, oats, barley and rye will show by the side of sugar cane, cotton and rice that she truly is able to yield the products of two zones. Cocoanuts and dates, figs and quinces, guavas and grapes, peaches and plums, pears and pineapples, tea and tobacco, citrons and shaddocks, limes and lemons, oranges and olives, cassava and celery, indigo and sisal hemp, ramie and alfalfa and every known vegetable will demonstrate the fertility of her soil and versatility of her products, while a 90lb watermelon will be there to show the Georgians what a real watermelon is. "Lives there a man with soul so dead" as not to be interested in that?

To the Tourist.

To see the orange groves, or what King Frost has left of them, visit the central, eastern, or western portions of the peninsula. There are no groves in northwestern Florida, in what might be called the pan-handle, or the toe of the inverted boot. Neither are there very extensive groves through the northern tier of counties. The groves down the west coast are of more recent growth, and while fine, are perhaps not so extensive or remarkable to see, as those along the upper St. Johns, particularly about Sanford, and DeLand—which nestles among them; and those on the Indian River—where one may walk through sixteen miles of continuous orange grove; and about what is known as the Lake Country. This region is seen in crossing the peninsula from Titusville to Tampa, by the J., T. & K. W. which passes through Leesburg, Apopka, Tavares and other towns, and skirts beautiful fresh water lakes, or by the Plant System, or by the South Florida R. R., all of which cross the State much of the way. On the East Coast orange culture has never flourished south of Sebastian. On the West Coast south of Tampa, particularly about Fort Myers, there are groves now loaded with fruit which did not drop their leaves from the freeze of '94-5. The rest of the orange region presents a sight, fair or sad to see, according to the amount of the gazer's hopefulness. The bark of the orange, when dry and dead, is pale gray in tint. Where they have been left untouched, the sight of the rows upon rows of almost silvery looking round-topped leafless trees, is very sad and most peculiar. They look like ghosts of groves. But, within the past few months they have taken on quite another aspect, somewhat that of resurrecting groves. All around the bases, and reaching up the trunks, pushing their way up through the central portions of the tree, are strong vigorous shoots, many of them 18 and 20 feet in length. They look now like immense green vases in which have been arranged light grasses. The interregnum of a year, or possibly two, will but whet the world's appetite for the Florida orange, and there will be plenty with which to satisfy.

The Pineapple Plantations.

For these in perfection follow the East Coast from Sebastian southward to Palm Beach. It is almost one continuous field for miles. For these take the East Coast Line.

On the St. Johns.

The Cocoanut Groves

Are found still farther south, on Lake Worth, and Biscayne Bay. Both pineapples and cocoanuts are found still farther south if one cares to visit the Keys or low lying coral islets skirting the southern coast of the peninsula. Key Largo and its products enjoy a world-wide fame. Take the same East Coast Line.

The Phosphate Mines.

The center of the phosphate region is Ocala. From this point the seeker can scarcely go astray. For the pebble or river phosphate he must go to the Peace River country, where Arcadia is the most accessible point, while Bartow and Brooksville claim rich deposits of bone phosphate. The geologist as well as the investor will find intense interest in all the western half of peninsular Florida. All this country is penetrated by the J., T. & K. W., and by the F. C. & P. R'y, and the Plant System.

The Sugar Plantations.

The sugar patch is seen waving its pale green foliage near every negro cabin and settler's home in the land, but the large plantations are the work of the Disston company at Kissimmee, where are grown stalks 30 feet long on lands reclaimed by drainage from the outer edges of the Everglades and the Okeechobee country. This is on the Florida Southern Road, a part of the Plant System.

The Tobacco Farms.

For these the traveller must take the F. C. & P. road, the only railway penetrating the western and northern portion of the State, to Quincy. Here is situated the great Owl Cigar Co.'s factory, besides several smaller factories. Tallahassee, also, has a large and flourishing factory, all supplied by the tobacco grown in Gadsden Co., in and around Quincy. Ybor City near Tampa is a city of 6,000 inhabitants made up entirely of tobacco factories and their employes, imported Cubans, and skilled laborers. For particulars see chapter on Tampa.

The Pear Orchards.

From fifty miles west of Jacksonville to the Alabama boundary the traveller sees no orange groves, but he sees acres upon acres of orchards, that have felt no drawback from the freeze. They are the LeConte and Kieffer pear orchards. The frost seemed to start them into new life. The present year they were overburdened with fruit. So abundant was the crop that thousands of bushels were left on the ground, to perish, or were fed to stock. The prices received did not pay the expense of shipping.

The Vegetable Farms.

For a model one may go to the home of Mr. U. J. White at Hastings, on the branch of the J., T. & K. W. connecting St. Augustine and Palatka. Or, leave the train at Lawtey, Starke, or almost any other town particularly in middle and western Florida, and strike out into the country in any direction.

Grapes.

For vineyards explore the region about Tallahassee, or visit Moultrie four miles from St. Augustine. Surprises await he who ventures.

SOME POINTERS
AS TO

Jacksonville, Florida.

(By CHARLES H. SMITH, Secretary of the Board of Trade.)

Its Advantages for Profitable Investment Are,

ITS LOCATION:—
At the head of ocean steam navigation on the St. Johns River, affording 1,000 miles of inland communication.

POPULATION 30,000—
Growing steadily; 10,000 increase in last five years.

ENTERPRISES—
Has Trolly cars, Gamewell fire alarm and paid fire department; Electric lights, pure Artesian water, well paved streets, good sewerage, fine public buildings, numerous churches and schools, public library, good banking facilities, six lines of steamers, eight railroad systems.

Business of $30,000,000 per annum.

Health excellent, mortality being but 10 in 1000.

FACTORIES—
Over 100 already in operation, but there is ample room for more. There is money to be made in the following, viz:

Canning Factories for the surplus vegetables, fruits, oysters, shrimp and fish. Potteries for the finest Kaolin in the world, of which the supply is inexhaustible. At the Atlanta Exposition will be shown 115 pieces of the finest egg-shell China, also specimens of ornamental tiling of this material. Tanneries to utilize the abundant saw palmetto which contains 11 to 12 per cent tannic acid, the leather tanned with which is as bright, durable, and gains as much as with oak or hemlock. The vast herds of native cattle in South Florida furnish the hides. The refuse of palmetto is 800 pounds per ton, and is valuable for paper stock, plastering hair, upholstering, cordage and cotton bagging.

WOOD-WORKING FACTORIES—
There are over 200 varieties of trees in Florida, of which but few have been utilized but pine and cypress. These woods are valuable for manufacturing into doors, sash and blinds, interior finish, cabinet work and furniture, cooperage, boat-building, wagons and carriages, agricultural implements, woodenware, baskets, cigar boxes, etc.

SOAP FACTORIES—
Materials for which are cheap and plentiful, viz: Tallow, cotton seed oil, etc.

CIGARS—
For the manufacture of which Jacksonville possesses superior advantages.

NAVAL STORE DEPOT—
Live men with capital can find no better location to control the turpentine and rosin now being produced extensively in the Florida pineries.

With cheap labor, a mild climate, ample transportation and plenty of raw materials, capital and brains only are essential to gain wealth.

For fuller particulars, address the Secretary of the Board of Trade.

Jacksonville.

The original name of this spot was Cow-ford. It was so known sixty years ago, at which time it was the ferry-point between the north and the south side of the St. John's river, by which the travel passed through the Spanish territory to that of the United States. While it was the ferry, it was also the point at which large numbers of cattle from South Florida, on the east side of the St. John's were made to swim or ford over, (if swimming may for convenience be called fording) under the guidance of the skilled boatmen, who led the van of the herd, encouraging it as a sort of nautical bell-wether, and sometimes holding the horn of a timid bovine, to a safe footing on the other side.

The Indian name for Cow-ford was Waccasasa, from the Spanish *vaca*, a cow. The Indian name for St. John's was Ouithlocko, corrupted by the white man's pronunciation to Withlaca, and finally by giving the Spanish sound of sharp *e* to the vowel *i*, it became Welaka. The Spanish name was San Juan; English, St. John.

Jacksonville, until the year 1816, never had a human habitation. In September of that year, the Spanish government made a grant of 200 acres of land lying north and east of McCoy's creek to Maria Taylor, widow of Purnal Taylor. She soon after married Lewis Z. Hogans, and removing to the north side of the river, cleared a place in the wilderness and built a home, opposite the present Everett Hotel.

Shortly after John Masters joined them as a neighbor.

John Brady became the third settler. Messrs. Dawson and Buckles built the first store. Mr. I. D. Hart kept the first boarding house, running it successfully for twenty

The Florida Finance Company.

115 Laura Street,

Jacksonville, Fla.

HAS FOR SALE

HOUSES and LOTS

In Jacksonville and Suburbs.

Also, Large and Small Tracts

Orange Groves and Wild Lands

In nearly all the Counties East of the Suwannee River.

Correspondence Solicited.
Terms and Prices to Suit the Times.

WILLIAM A. DELL,
DISPENSING CHEMIST,

BAY, COR. LAURA STREET,

Jacksonville, Fla.

ALL GOODS AT

CUT PRICES.

Special attention given to Family Trade throughout the State.

years. John L. Doggett was the first judge of the county court.

The town was laid out in 1822 by Messrs. Hogans, Brady & Hart. The streets were made seventy feet wide. Bay St. was made eighty feet wide. It was given the name Jacksonville by Col. Warren, an enthusiastic admirer of Old Hickory.

The first county court was held in 1822, with George Gibbs, clerk; James Dell, sheriff, and D. C. Hart, deputy.

The first United States Court was held in Dec. 1823, with Hon. J. L. Smith, father of Gen. Kirby Smith, as judge. In 1835 was published the first newspaper, *The Courier*.

In 1850 it had 400 inhabitants; in 1860, it had 2,000; in 1894, its population was 28,000.

In 1858, under the direction of Gen. W. M. Ledwith, and Dr. A. S. Baldwin, an old negro, April Sauriz, planted the live-oak and water-oak trees that now line the streets in the older portions of Jacksonville.

The Jacksonville of to-day is a busy, thriving, hustling metropolis of a rapidly growing State. It occupies eight and a half square miles. It is the largest city in the State. Its population is nearly 30,000. It is the terminus of six railways, and two others are projected. Four ocean steamer lines afford regular and direct communication with New York, Philadelphia and Baltimore. It is the gateway to Florida, the Bahamas and Cuba. It is located on the noble St. Johns river, which, with its tributaries, gives 1,000 miles of inland navigation. The city has nine miles of river frontage. The United States Government has expended over $1,000,000 in constructing jetties at the mouth of the river, and the County of Duval has expended $300,000 in deepening the channel, so that now there is eighteen feet of water from Jacksonville to the Ocean. The government is now making surveys with a view of obtaining a channel twenty-four feet deep.

Being only fourteen miles from the Atlantic and one

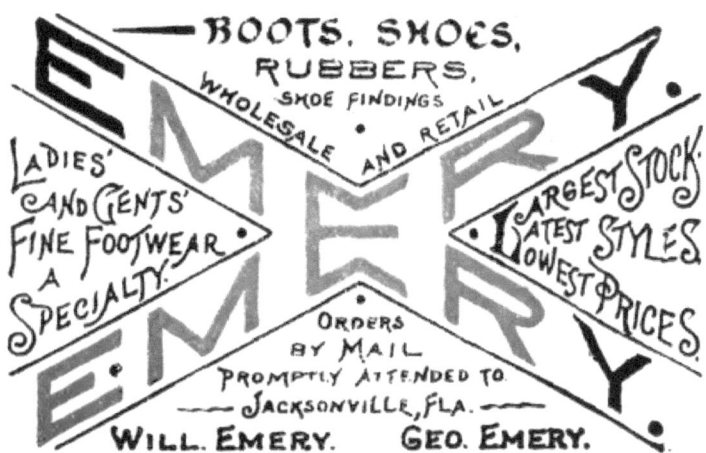

HOTEL PLACIDE,

N. L. WARD, PROPRIETOR.

Main Street, - - - JACKSONVILLE, FLA

ONE BLOCK FROM BAY.

OPEN ALL THE YEAR.

THE PLACIDE is a new building, completed December, 1886. Its construction and appliances are all of modern design and finish. The sanitary arrangements are excellent, the plumbing being thorough and systematic and drainage perfect. The Hotel is newly furnished with exceptionally fine furniture throughout, and is, without doubt, the best hotel in the city. The rooms are arranged either singly or in suites, and as many bedrooms as desired. The house having and eastern and southern exposure, the rooms are light, airy and cheerful. Open fire places in nearly every room in the house.

The cuisine is all that could be desired, our cooks are the best that can be obtained; every possible attention will be given to the dining-room, and nothing will be omitted which can contribute to the health and comfort of the guests.

TERMS—$2.50 to $4.00 Per Day. Special Rates Weekly and to Families.

Baggage checked to all points direct from the hotel. Bus meets all trains.

SAMPLE ROOM FREE.

THE GEO. W. CLARK COMPANY.

Mantels,
Grates,
AND
Tiling
FROM
$4 to $150.

FIVE
CATALOGUES.

IRON FENCING
AT
LOWEST PRICES

BICYCLES,
LAWN MOWERS

We Manufacture and Do a Wholesale Business.

Monuments
and
Headstones

FROM
$15 to $5,000.

Agents Wanted Everywhere.

Address,

**50 BEEKMAN STREET,
NEW YORK.**
AND JACKSONVILLE, FLORIDA.

hundred miles from the Gulf of Mexico, the city is always cooled by ocean or gulf breezes, so that even in summer Jacksonville is a comfortable place in which to live. It is only thirty minutes by rail from one of the finest ocean beaches in the United States.

It is the commercial emporium and business metropolis of Florida. There are ten banks.

The wholesale and retail houses carry heavy stocks of goods, in their respective lines, hence they are enabled to compete successfully with their northern rivals whose drummers are continually canvassing the State. By their energy and wise liberality they have built up a trade of over forty millions per annum.

The size and general fine appearance of the stores and shops on Bay street are a matter of surprise and gratification to all visitors. To visit some of the china and queensware stores, with their carefully selected, artistic wares, is like strolling through an art gallery.

The establishment of Messrs. Greenleaf & Crosby is rapidly acquiring a national reputation. It is the Tiffany's of the Southeast. Although their most extensive trade is in jewelry and diamonds, their stock of bric-a-brac, cut-glass ware and fine art goods generally, is perhaps unequaled south of New York. A member of this firm visits Europe every year, and their goods are selected in the art centers of the world. Many of their designs in jewelry and silverware are original and characteristic, and have attained immediate and surprising popularity.

They have branch houses at St. Augustine and Palm Beach.

Jacksonville's commerce is shown by the fact that in 1894 the average tonnage was 1,060 and sailing vessels of 450 tons or more are common visitors to her wharves. Since the deepening of the river channel to fifteen feet, mean low water, by the expenditure of $300,000, vessels drawing sixteen feet and eight inches can come and go with safety.

JACKSONVILLE'S ONLY FIRE-PROOF HOTEL
HOTEL GENEVA.

COR. FORSYTH AND CEDAR STS.
COMPLETED IN 1895. MODERN IMPROVEMENTS. BATHS ETC. ON EVERY FLOOR. GAS & ELECTRIC LIGHTS. PASSENGER ELEVATOR
$2.50 TO 4.00 .. SHARP FAMILY - PROS.

ARTISTICALLY & ELEGANTLY FURNISHED

CORONADO. SURF-BATHING THE YEAR ROUND

SHARP FAMILY - OWNERS, PROPRIETORS.
OPP. NEW SMYRNA - FLA

20 MILES OF BEACH FOR A PLAY-GROUND !!

Dr. W. T. S. Vincent, whose likeness is here shown, is well known throughout the United States and Canada as the originator of the most advanced and successful of treatments for Chronic Diseases, and especially noted as the originator of the

IMPERIAL RUPTURE CURE.

This grand treatment is Safe, Speedy, Painless and Permanent. No Operation, No Cutting, No Detention from Business. No Cure, No Pay

W. T. S. VINCENT, M. D.,
SPECIALIST.

All curable cases of Catarrh, Nose, Throat and Lung diseases, Eye, Ear, Stomach, Liver and Kidneys, Gravel, Rheumatism, Paralysis, Neuralgia, Nervous and Heart diseases, Blood and Skin diseases, Consumption in early stages, diseases of Bladder and Female Organs, Sexual Weakness and Private diseases skillfully treated. Persons unable to visit the doctors should send for symptom blank, enabling them to take home treatment.

We undertake no incurable cases, but cure thousands given up to die. Consultation Free and Confidential.

Headquarters 36 Main Street, Jacksonville, Florida.

W. M. Bostwick, Jr.,
ATTORNEY AT LAW.

2½ East Bay St.,   JACKSONVILLE,
Room 5.   FLORIDA.

COLLECTIONS.   TAXES PAID.

M. A. Brown,
ATTORNEY AT LAW.

Law Exchange,   Jacksonville,
21 Market Street.   Florida

G. P. HALL.   T. HILDITCH.   A. S. RUSSELL.

HALL, HILDITCH & CO.,

Will give prompt attention to your orders for

WALL PAPER AND PAINTS,
PICTURE FRAMES and MOULDING,
PAPER HANGING and PAINTING,

26 West Forsyth Street,   JACKSONVILLE, FLA.

Best materials and workmanship in both branches. Estimates given and satisfaction guaranteed.

THE FLORIDA TIMES-UNION,

OFFICE: TELEPHONES:
Cor. Bay and Laura Sts.   Editorial Rooms 182, Bus. Office 40

JACKSONVILLE, FLA.

The First Established and Always the Leading Daily in the State.

THE ONLY DAILY

South of Savannah having the Associated Press Dispatches.

The Daily Florida Times-Union

IS ISSUED EVERY MORNING.

Terms, $10.00 a Year; $5.00 Six Months; $2.50 Three Months.

It has the exclusive Southern Associated and United Press Franchises. Receiving specials from all quarters on important topics, and has correspondents in all the leading news centers of the country.

The Evening Times-Union,

Issued Daily, Sundays Excepted.   Ten Cents Per Week.

The Semi-Weekly Times-Union,

(Semi-Weekly edition of the Daily Times-Union.)

Issued every Tuesday and Friday; containing all the news, State and general, and a great variety of interesting reading, including farm and household matters. With the growing interest in Florida everywhere, the Semi-Weekly is rapidly attaining a universal circulation.

Mailed, postage free, for One Dollar per year.

Specimen copies free to any address.

One of the best advertising mediums anywhere.

Jacksonville has over 100 factories of various kinds, employing an aggregate capital of a million and one-half of dollars. There is room still for the profitable employment of more capital in Jacksonville. The abundant raw palmetto contains more tannic acid than any known tree or plant except the oak. Careful analysis shows eleven to twelve per cent. Herds of native cattle abound in South Florida, the hides from which are shipped to the North and the leather returned to Florida. A tannery would pay. The refuse is worth more than the green raw material. There are 800 pounds of fibre to the ton, which can be utilized for paper stock, plastering hair, bedding and upholstering material, cordage, oakum, felt, or in lieu of jute for cotton bagging. Soap factories can find abundant material and a good market. Money can be made from the canning of vegetables, fruits, oysters and shrimp. Lime can be made from shell and rock. The lumber that has thus far been manufactured is chiefly from pine and cypress, but there are over 200 species of wood that have scarcely been touched. Cotton mills located here would be in close proximity to the cotton fields of Florida, Georgia and Alabama.

Its mortality averages only ten in a thousand, the lowest in the United States. Artesian wells supply the city with 5,000,000 gallons daily of pure water.

An efficient paid fire department is its safeguard against extensive conflagrations; and it has a well organized police department.

Its numerous fine hotels afford ample accommodation to thousands of tourists.

Its forty-eight churches; its numerous public and private schools; its kindergarten; its public free library; its four daily and ten weekly newspapers; its two luxurious clubhouses; its numerous lodges; its excellent markets, and its fine opera house enables the average citizen to extract as much comfort from life as in greater and more pretentious cities.

The C. C. Robertson
Real Estate Agency,

N. E. Cor. Bay and Main Sts.,
Over L'Engle's Drug Store,

Telephone 184.

Jacksonville, Florida.

ORANGE GROVES, + TIMBER TRACTS,

Improved or Unimproved Property for Sale or Exchange.

Money Lending a Specialty.

Several large tracts of Timber and Colony site properties, Phosphate Lands, both improved and unimproved, at great bargains.

Parties having large interests in other States, desiring to exchange same for Florida property, should see us.

J. D. Bucky's Sons,

The Shoe Hustlers.

Highest Quality,
Best Value,
Any Styles.

33 W. Bay Street,
Jacksonville, Fla.

Agents Hanan & Son, New York.

Among its public buildings are a fine U. S. Custom House and Postoffice which cost nearly $300,000. The Duval County Court House cost $100,000. The Union building erected by the Board of Trade, City Library, and B. and P. Order of Elks. The Seminole Club building, the Masonic Temple and the Odd Fellows Hall.

The railroads centering here have a capacious union depot. Twelve miles of electric railway have been built, and a magificent railroad bridge spans the St. Johns River. Hundreds of private dwellings have been and are now being erected and a new era of prosperity has dawned upon the city.

Florida is now attracting thousands of emigrants to whom a few words of advice from the Board of Trade may be apropos.

To The Settler.

WHO SHOULD AND WHO SHOULD NOT SETTLE IN FLORIDA. Don't go empty handed. A little capital is just as necessary to get a start in Florida as anywhere else.

Don't go if you are doing well where you are. Florida is no place for discontented folks.

Don't go expecting to find a country where you can live with little or no work, unless you have an income that will support you.

Don't go if you are out of a job and can't get one at home. If you can't find employment where you are known you will not be likely to find it among strangers.

Don't go if you are a semi-invalid hoping to earn enough to pay expenses during the winter and then return to the North in the spring. Florida is full of such deluded unfortunates.

Don't go if you are merely the "promoter" of a "splendid business scheme" with the expectation of finding capitalists ready to put up the cash against your "experience" and pay you a fat salary as manager of a company.

JOHN L. MARVIN,   H. T. BAYA,   T. W. CONRAD,
President.   Cashier.   Assistant Cashier.

Merchants National Bank
OF JACKSONVILLE, FLA.

Capital, $100,000.00.

SURPLUS AND UNDIVIDED PROFITS
$20,000.00.

Fire and Burglar-Proof Vaults.

The accounts of individuals and mercantile firms, as well as those of banks and bankers, are solicited, and will receive every attention consistent with conservative management.

SAFETY DEPOSIT BOXES TO RENT.

THE FLORIDA CITIZEN,

An Eight-Page Daily Newspaper, Devoted to the Interests of the State of Florida.

Published Every Day in the Year.

SUBSCRIPTION RATES:

One year, by mail	$5.00
Six months, by mail	ial 1.00
Three months, by mail	2.00
One month, by mail	.65

☞ Delivered by carrier within the limits of the city of Jacksonville for eight cents a month additional.

WEEKLY FLORIDA CITIZEN,
PUBLISHED EVERY THURSDAY.

Subscription rate, by mail................................ One Dollar per Year.

☞ All subscriptions are payable in advance.

315 West Bay Street,   = =   JACKSONVILLE, FLA.

Go if you have capital to lend or invest in any legitimate manufacturing enterprise.

Go if you are plucky and energetic, and know how to embrace an opportunity when you see it.

Go if you like a mild climate better than a cold one—a good "all the year round" climate.

Go if you are a horticulturist, vine grower, truck gardener or a good mechanic.

Go if you are willing to assist in developing the wonderful resources of the State and become a permanent citizen.

To the Tourist.

Jacksonville has been called a city of hotels. Of these, the following are the leading:

PROPRIETOR	NAME OF HOUSE	CAPACITY	RATES PER DAY	RATES PER WEEK
J. R. Campbell	St. James	500	$4.00	$21.00
Warren	Windsor Hotel	600	$4 and upward	$21.00
J. Leland				
J. B. Baker	Everett Hotel	300	$3.00	Special

These rank first, and every winter are filled with the wealthiest and most noted of this and other nations. Their registers often bear the most distinguished of living names.

The St. James and the Windsor face the city park and while near the Opera House and livery stables, are removed from the noise and bustle of the business part of the town.

The first-named occupies an entire block, and is bounded by four streets. Its proprietor was a pioneer hotel man in Florida, and has seen the town grow from an unpaved village. He has a reputation that is national, and counts all his guests as friends.

The Everett is on Bay street, at its busiest point. Its windows look out upon the river at its principal docks, the viaduct, and the railway rendezvous. It is in the heart of business.

The Windsor and Everett occupy each one half a block. They have been recently renovated and largely refurnished. See cards on another page.

ESTABLISHED 1887.

THE METROPOLIS,

The Recognized Evening Newspaper in Florida.

IT GIVES ALL THE SOCIETY, LOCAL, STATE AND MARINE NEWS OF THE DAY.

Has the Exclusive Franchise of the Union Associated Press Reports.

AS AN ADVERTISING MEDIUM IT HAS NO SUPERIOR IN THE STATE.

☞ Circulation of a newspaper can always be judged by its advertisers. You will find the leading business men of Jacksonville as advertisers in this paper.

SUBSCRIPTION PRICE, IN ADVANCE:

Daily, one year .... $4.00 Daily, three months $1.00
Daily, six months .... 2.00 *Saturday Edition*, one year .... 50c.

☞ Advertising rates furnished on application.

The Saturday Evening Metropolis.

A six-column, eight-page quarto, giving all the latest news of the day, together with a number of stories and miscellaneous topics of the day.
Advertising rates furnished on application for this edition.

☞ Address all communications to   CARTER & RUSSELL,
Metropolis Building, - - - - - - Jacksonville.

Florida Farmer and Fruit-Grower.

ESTABLISHED 1869.

THE FOREMOST EXPONENT OF THE NATURAL WEALTH AND THE cultural possibilities of Florida. Though devoted mainly to citrus culture as the one pre-eminent industry which will ever distinguish this Commonwealth among all the States of the Union, the one attraction which gives her distinction and brings her colonists from all the countries of Christendom, at the same time this journal does not neglect those branches of soil culture which, while less celebrated, are none the less useful and profitable.

To every member of the English-speaking race who migrates to a semi-tropical land, rural life presents a great number of untried and novel conditions which must be mastered thoroughly to insure success. Nowhere else where Anglo Saxon colonists have settled do they so urgently require the guidance and instruction of a good agricultural journal as in sub-tropical regions.

THE

Farmer and Fruit-Grower is Published Weekly

AT $2 A YEAR.

Address   THE PUBLISHER,

JACKSONVILLE, FLA.

Other hotels, quite their equals possibly in comforts, are:

PROPRIETOR	NAME OF HOUSE	CAPACITY	RATES PER DAY	RATES PER WEEK
N. L. Ward	Placide	150	$2.50 to $4.00	$12.50 and up.
The Sharpe Family	Geneva	75	$2.50 to $4.00	Special.
Crapo & LeVene	Carlton	200	$2.50 to $3.00	$10 to $17.50
Dodge & Cullen	New Duval			
G. W. Smith	Grand View	200	$2.50 to $3.00	Special.
Mrs. Hudnall	St. Johns House			

These are all situated in and near the business centres of the town. The Placide is on Main street, one block from Bay, on the Main street trolley line, very desirably located. It is a new building completed less than two years ago. It has all modern appliances and perfect sanitary arrangements. Its furnishings are exceptionally fine. The rooms may be had singly or *en suite*, with open fire-places in every room. With an energetic, progressive proprietor of much experience, and with the best cuisine, this house is a large success. It is open all the year. (For rates, etc., see card.)

The Geneva is much nearer the depots, wharfs and docks. It is one block from Bay street, and nearer the rapidly growing western portion of the city. It has been entirely overhauled, re-decorated and furnished, and is in the hands of experienced hotel people.

The Carlton, New Duval and St. John's House are all-the-year hotels.

The following furnish rooms only:

		CAPACITY	RATES FOR ROOMS
The Acme	On West Bay	100	50c to $1.00
The Travelers	On West Bay	100	50c to $1.00
The Bristol	On East Bay	45	$3.00 per week
The Oxford	Opp. St. James	60	

The Warner House on Laura street, in one of the most beautiful residence portions of the city, and Hotel Roseland in the extreme eastern portion of the town, on the banks of the St. John's river, are cosy, quiet, carefully-kept family hotels of moderate size with reasonable rates.

Savings and Trust Bank of Florida,

JACKSONVILLE.

CAPITAL $50,000.

H. ROBINSON, President.   W. J. HARKISHEIMER, Vice-Pres.
WM. RAWLINSON, Cashier.

DIRECTORS

H. Robinson,   J. Hildebrandt,   P. E. McMurray,
W. J. Harkisheimer,   Philip Walter,   R. H. Liggett,
J. A. Henderson,   C. C. Robertson,   W. B. Owen.

Collections made on all points of Florida, and remitted for on day of payment.

Active and Savings Accounts Solicited. Interest Paid on Savings.

McMURRAY'S
TRANSFER
AND JACKSONVILLE
LIVERY
AND SALE STABLES.
1527 Newman St.,
Opp. Tremont Hotel.

JACKSONVILLE CLUB STABLES.
Cor. Bay and Cedar.

HORSES, BUGGIES, PHAETONS AND OTHER VEHICLES
CONSTANTLY FOR HIRE.

HORSES AND MULES FOR SALE.
Boarding Horses a Specialty.

THOMAS McMURRAY, Proprietor,
Jacksonville, Fla.

IF YOU SHAVE YOURSELF
A FINE RAZOR IS A NECESSITY.

We will mail you one guaranteed to require no honing, post paid on receipt of $1.25.

SATISFACTION GUARANTEED.

R. J. MARTINEZ, Jacksonville, Fla.

A method of living in Jacksonville, much in favor among those who wish to be untrammeled by the formalities of hotel life, is to rent furnished rooms and take meals at convenient boarding houses or restaurants near by. In bad weather, or for invalids, the meals may be sent to such rooms.

Still another method, which to many recommends itself as economical, is to rent an empty room, and furnish it to suit one's own taste and convenience with furniture rented for the purpose by the month or week. Furniture may be thus hired, and returned when desired, from any furniture house in the city. The large establishment of the Cleaveland Furniture Co. on West Forsyth street near the Geneva Hotel, or Fetting & Co. on East Bay street, have large stocks and sell or rent at New York prices. Crockery, kerosene or gasolene stoves of every size and description, and all other necessaries for light housekeeping may be obtained at the same place. See cards.

The principal boarding houses are:

Mrs. Henderson's, on Main street, near Monroe.

Mrs. Slager's, next door to Mrs. Henderson's, is a Jewish house, where all Israelites put up. It is stylish and first-class, but exclusively Hebrew.

Mrs. Chapman's, next corner north of St. James Hotel.

Mrs. McGowan's, corner Laura and Beaver streets.

Mrs. Ochus, on Ocean street, two blocks from Bay street.

Mrs. Starke, corner Forsyth and Laura streets.

Mrs. Rich, one block west of St. James.

Mrs. Fleming's, on Monroe street, three blocks from Bay street and one block west of Carleton Hotel.

All these houses are well kept, most of them with much elegance and by refined ladies, and are in all respects preferable to a small hotel. They are open all the year round, and are kept more specially for local patronage, although almost any of them will admit a few winter visitors.

Almost any comfortably established family will accom-

ISEMAN & CLAUSSEN,

WHOLESALE

Commission Merchants,

Fruits and Produce.

NOS. 220-222 Bay Street,

JACKSONVILLE, FLA.

FURNIIURE

CARPETS ❖ MATTINGS

COOKING STOVES

OAK MANTLES AND FIREPLACE GOODS, ETC.

The Largest Assortment South,

Our Wareroom Covers 36,000 Sq. Ft. Floor Space.

Special Low Prices to New Comers Coming into the State.

SPECIAL DISCOUNT.

We are known as the Old Reliable. Established nearly 20 years ago.

With low prices and strict business principles our success has been phenomenal.

The Cleaveland Furniture Company,

415 to 427 W. Forsyth Street,
  (Next to Geneva Hotel.)

Jacksonville, Florida.

modate an invalid or a tourist, who prefers the quiet of a private house to a hotel. Their rates are reasonable, seldom more than seven dollars per week; often, but five.

The strict sanitary laws of the city compel such close attention to drainage, sewerage, etc., that almost without exception all private houses have all modern improvements, as bath rooms, pure water, and the like.

To the Invalid.

Jacksonville has many fine physicians of all schools. Among the allopathic physicians whose reputation is unquestioned are Drs. Drew, Daniels, Livingston, Williams, Mitchell, Matthews, Wakefield and others.

Homœopathy is well represented in the persons of Dr. H. B. Stout, and Drs. Johnson, Sr. and Jr. As surgeons, Dr. Matthews, Dr. Livingston, and Dr. Williams enjoy high reputations.

Of first-class druggists, and finely equipped drug stores, Jacksonville has her full quota. In the first rank is the large and elegantly fitted up establishment of W. A. Dell, corner Bay and Laura streets. Another, and a great favorite is that of Gilbert Williams cor. of Bay and Laura streets. In the western part of Bay street, is the accomplished druggist R. Martinez, who may be found at the foot of the viaduct, on the corner of Bay and Bridge streets.

The livery stables of this city would be creditable to a town of 100,000 inhabitants. McMurray's stables corner of Forsyth and Newnan streets are equipped with some of the finest turnouts in the South.

Thebaut's stables on Julia street are conveniently near the St. James and Windsor Hotels.

To the Investor.

He who wishes to inquire into the business opportunities, or status in Jacksonville, or the surrounding country, or indeed of the State, may safely and freely consult Mr. C. C. Robertson. They are sure of a careful hearing,

THE ST. JAMES,

JACKSONVILLE, - - FLORIDA.

SEASON 1895-6.   WILL OPEN NOVEMBER 28, 1895.

THE ST. JAMES needs no introduction to visitors to Florida. From a small beginning in 1869, The St. James has increased in size and added to its appointments with the increasing popularity of the tourist's travel to Florida.

The St. James is to-day the equal, if not the superior, of any hotel in Jacksonville and has all the arrangements for the comfort of its guests. Electric bells, electric lights, steam heat in halls and public rooms, bath rooms, *en suite*, elevator, broad stairways, etc., have been provided. There is also over seven hundred feet of veranda for promenade.

The location is unsurpassed, being on the highest ground in Jacksonville, facing the St. James Park.

It has accommodations for five hundred guests. The table is supplied with carefully filtered rain water, absolutely pure, with artificial ice made from distilled water; and the choicest meats, fruits and vegetables from Northern and Southern markets.

There is a ticket office in the hotel where tickets are sold and baggage checked to all points North.

Its Music, as in past seasons, will be furnished by Prof. Ed. Prouty's Orchestra, and will be of high grade. Address by mail or telegraph.

J. R. CAMPBELL, Prop.   C. O. CHAMBERLIN, M'gr.
Jacksonville, Florida.

Photographs may be seen and information given in New York at The Outlook Recreation Department, 13 Astor Place.

courteous attention, perfectly reliable information, and his own pronounced success is proof sufficient of the wisdom of his judgment, and the safety of his advice.

Mr. A. W. Barrs is another well informed and thoroughly reliable dealer.

In real estate in and about the city, J. C. Greeley & Co. are among the most extensive dealers.

Pleasant Places in and About Jacksonville.

The pleasantest short drives about Jacksonville are through the beautiful suburbs of Springfield and Riverside. Both these places are penetrated with trolley lines. For the first, take the Main street electric car; for the latter, take Riverside car on Bay street. The round trip on either is a pleasant half hour's recreation. Carriages may be hired from hackmen on the street for $1.00 per hour. T. McMurray on Newnan street, two doors from Bay street, has a fine livery stable, where may be obtained stylish turnouts of all descriptions, fine saddle horses, and skilled drivers, all at reasonable prices. Mr. McMurray has all a thorough horseman's love of fine animals and keeps no others about him. (See his card on another page).

With a hack, the drive through Springfield may be continued to Evergreen Cemetery, and beyond it, circling the city in what is known as the nine-mile shell drive, returning through the eastern portion of the city, by Duval street, which is smoothly paved, and unobstructed by street car lines, or by Bay street, which is as animated and gay in a winter afternoon as the boulevards of Paris.

Points on the River.

On the St. John's some lovely places to visit are the elegant homes, on the south side of the river, opposite the city. A row or sail boat may be obtained at the boat-yard near the Yacht Club House at the foot of Market street for about twenty-five cents an hour. Skilled oarsmen or

OCEAN STEAMSHIP COMPANY.

Savannah * Line.

G. M. SORREL, Manager.

The Ships of this Line are Appointed to Sail from

SAVANNAH TO NEW YORK

On Tuesdays, Fridays and Sundays.

FROM SAVANNAH TO BOSTON

EVERY THURSDAY.

Fare between Savannah and New York, $25 for First Class, $19 for Intermediate, $43.30 for Round Trip.

☛ The Ship from Savannah to Philadelphia, the *Dessong*, does not carry passengers.

sailors are easily engaged for twenty-five cents per hour each. Yachts and naphtha launches may be hired for $1 per hour, fully manned. The row or sail across the river is a delight.

On the opposite shore two miles up the river is Villa Alexandria, the home of Mrs. Alexander Mitchell, widow of the late Alexander Mitchell, the railroad king of Milwaukee, and a few years since the Vanderbilt of the northwest. This place is reckoned among the noted beautiful homes of America. The approach from the river is particularly beautiful.

Two or three miles down the river is the Cummings' place, a home founded by the late Asa Packer, of Pennsylvania, now owned by his sister and heir, Mrs. Cummings. Another place in the same vicinity, most picturesquely situated, is the winter home of Gen. Divens of Elmira, New York. Other homes of great beauty are dotted along the banks for miles.

To those who do not like the water, there is another way of reaching these points. A ferry boat leaves the wharf at the foot of Newnan street every half hour. A hack or other vehicle can cross on this boat, and a pleasant drive of two miles over a shelled road, ends at the rear entrance and porter's lodge of Villa Alexandria. At certain seasons, visitors are allowed to drive through these enchanting grounds, on all days except Sundays.

A pleasant river road leads to the other places mentioned.

A delightful river excursion is a trip on one of the St. John's river steamers to Green Cove Springs, Magnolia, Palatka and other points up the river. The trip to Green Cove, Mandarin and Magnolia may be accomplished in a day, if most of the time be spent on the river. Only brief visits are afforded at each point. A more satisfactory way is to spend a few days at Green Cove or Magnolia, which are within walking distance of each other, and both of

M. F. GATELY,
Cheap Cash Grocery,
NO. 504 MAIN STREET.
JACKSONVILLE, FLA.

FRESH GROCERIES, CANNED GOODS.

FRUITS AND VEGETABLES.

ESTABLISHED 1883.
NEW YORK STEAM LAUNDRY.
26 OCEAN ST., NEAR BAY.
JACKSONVILLE, FLORIDA.

F. E. SMITH, Proprietor.

CALDWELL & SCOTT,
WHOLESALE

Coffees, Teas, Spices AND Grocer's Sundries.

111 Main Street.   JACKSONVILLE, FLORIDA.

TELEPHONE NO. 11.   ESTABLISHED 1870   TIME TRIED AND FIRE TESTED.

J. H. NORTON,
(Attorney at Law.)

NORTHWEST COR. BAY AND OCEAN STS., - JACKSONVILLE, FLA.

FIRE INSURANCE.

Representing Leading American and English Companies.

YOUR BUSINESS SOLICITED.

☞ Refers to Patrons who have had losses during the past twenty-five years.

which have excellent hotels. The fare is cheap, the hotels $2.00 and $3.00 houses, and the trip, in toto, an inexpensive but delightful one.

To those who wish a glimpse of the Atlantic, the railroad to Pablo, a local summer seaside resort, with a wonderful beach, offers an opportunity. Take ferry at foot of Newnan street and train from depot on opposite side of the river. Or, either steamer or train will carry the traveller to Mayport, at the mouth of the St. John's river. Take steamer at foot of Main street or train from Pablo depot, across the river. Fine surf bathing at Pablo, and incomparable fishing at Mayport. At Burnside, on the Atlantic beach, between the two points, is a hotel.

From Jacksonville, the tourist who wishes to make a trip of the State, before he leaves it, will be forced to make a choice of routes.

He may go down the eastern coast closely hugging the Atlantic shore until Biscayne Bay, his utmost limit, is reached. Thence he must return nearly half the way to Titusville, and from there swing in long graceful curves across the peninsula to Tampa on the Gulf Coast. From this point, he can turn northward through the western counties until he reaches the northern portions of the State. Here he may turn westward and traverse what may be called the pan-handle of the State, retracing his steps and arriving again in Jacksonville.

Or, with equally good results, he may reverse this

I LEAD; OTHERS FOLLOW.

GILBERT W. WILLIAMS,
"THE DRUGGIST,"

Bay Street, Corner Hogan,   JACKSONVILLE, FLORIDA.

PROMPT AND PERSONAL ATTENTION TO ALL PRESCRIPTION WORK. ONLY THE FINEST CHEMICALS USED.

REDUCED RATES TO ALL POINTS.

MAYNARD'S TICKET AGENCY

(Member American Ticket Brokers' Association.)

FELIX GARCIA, Manager,

201 West Bay Street - - Cor. Bay and Hogan.

JACKSONVILLE, FLORIDA.

FLORIDA TOURS.

ATLANTA OFFICE, 7 N. PRYOR ST., OPP. THE "KIMBALL."   TAMPA OFFICE, 313 FRANKLIN ST.

THIS HANDSOME

Oak Rocker,

Upholstered in Silk Plush.

ONLY $3.50.

—*OTHERS AT*—

$2.75, $3, $4, $6,

AND UP, AT

E. M. FETTING'S

FURNITURE STORE,

14 East Bay Street,

JACKSONVILLE, FLA.

itinerary, and go first to the extreme western end of the State, return to within less than one hundred miles of Jacksonville, then veer southward parallel with the western or gulf coast of the peninsula, turning eastward, and by the East Coast Line return to Jacksonville.

For many reasons, it were well perhaps to take the first as a typical route.

The first objective point would be

FLORIDA EAST COAST HOTEL SYSTEM

C. B. KNOTT, General Superintendent.

ST. AUGUSTINE.

HOTEL PONCE DE LEON.

GILLIS & MURRAY, ... Managers.
Rate, $5.00 and upward per day.
Open January to April.

HOTEL ALCAZAR.

Jos. P. Graves, ... Manager.
Rate, $3.00 and upward per day.
Open November to May.

HOTEL CORDOVA.

Rooms Only.   February and March.

HOTEL ORMOND.

Anderson & Price, ... Managers.
Open January 11 to April.
Rate, $4.00 and upward per day.

HOTEL ROYAL POINCIANA.

H. W. Merrill, ... Manager.
Rate, $5.00 and upward per day.
January 20 to April.

PALM BEACH INN.

Fred Sterry, ... Manager.
Rate, $4.00 and upward per day.
Open December to May.

St. Augustine.

Distance from Jacksonville 38 miles. Fare $1.50. Round Trip, $3.00. Take East Coast Railway at Union Depot. Ticket office in Transportation Row on West Bay street, between Hogan and Julia streets.

It has been said that the three most interesting places on this continent are Santa Fe, Toronto and St. Augustine. Whatever may be said of the other two, St. Augustine has largely occupied the public eye for the last few years.

It has ever been a point of historical interest, as the first settled town in America. The old fort looked over the bay, the Spanish grandee strode with jingling spurs through the narrow streets, watched by dark-eyed senoritas from the overhanging balconies above; the devout priest passed to the old cathedral, and black-robed nuns glided within the convent doors, more than half a century before the hymns of the Puritans waked the echoes of the New England woods, or the wassail songs of the Dutch rang sturdily over the swamps of Manhattan Island. With all this, here is to-day the same old fort, intact, complete, impregnable. The same cathedral simply restored after its partial destruction by fire; the same chime of bells in the tower calls the devout to morning mass or evening vespers, that summoned worshipers before William Penn had ever seen an Indian. Deep cast in their sides is the story of their age—1683. Three centuries old! and the cathedral in which they hang antedates them by a score of years.

If the town were dilapidated, repulsive and inaccessible this historic interest would call a full quota of visitors. But when, added to this, we find that the place was originally modeled after the cramped little towns that nestle in narrow valleys among Castilian mountains, or close under the crags of a sea-cliff, on a Spanish coast; that it was built of almost imperishable material, and stands to-day, a typical foreign town on American soil, with all the dignity, but none of the decrepitude of extreme old age, it then becomes a magnet of wondrous power, and its visitors number thousands each year.

Mrs. Stowe, on her first visit, remarked that it seems as if some sleepy old town in sunny Spain, had broken loose from its moorings, and slipping into the Atlantic, had stranded on the American shore, leaving its overlooking castle behind.

Within the past ten years, however, a change has come over the dreamy old town. Modern capital and enterprise has supplied the missing castle—a structure more suitable for a king's palace than for any other use. With a good taste that is an inspiration, this building that contains every convenience and luxury of modern ingenuity, is built in such complete harmony with its ancient surroundings that there is no jar or discord in the whole.

Nothing in America, and not many things in Europe, can approach in architectural beauty and magnificence of design, the group of Spanish-Moresque Palaces, the Hotels Ponce de Leon, Alcazar and Cordova. On one side the park-like grounds, sparkling fountains, tropical verdure and blooming plants mark the entrance grounds of one hotel. The round tower, the kneeling balconies, the wide parapets of a mediæval castle, gives a mere intimation of the dimensions of another. At the left a gate-way, lofty, arched and grand in proportions, as rich in its finishings and as imposing in its entirety as any of the triumphal arches of foreign cities. Through this arched gate-way, entrance is had to the enclosed court of the Hotel Ponce de Leon, blooming at all times of the year with fragrance and beauty. This wonderful building is a monolith, practically one single stone. It has been molded from the concrete of

Hotel Ponce de Leon—St. Augustine, Fla.

Exchanging Northern Property for Southern a Specialty

J. H. SLATER,

✻ABSTRACTER.✻

REAL ESTATE AND LOAN AGENT,

ST. AUGUSTINE, - FLORIDA.

"THE VALENCIA,"

OPEN FROM NOVEMBER 1st, TO MAY 30th

ST. AUGUSTINE, FLA.

MRS. MARY FRAZER, Proprietress.

CONSTRUCTED by the builders of the Ponce de Leon, the Valencia embodies the most perfect hotel arrangements of the day. All is homelike and comfortable within, and the broad verandas overlook spacious grounds, beautiful with the orange, the rose and the palm. The house is delightfully situated, on St. George street, south of the Plaza. It is conducted by Mrs. Mary Frazer, whose successful management has been known to so many St. Augustine visitors during the past fifteen years.

which it is built. It is almost time-proof, entirely fire-proof, and so firm and solid that it would nonplus an earthquake. From turret to foundation stone there is no sham, no imitation. All is solid massive stone, genuine terra cotta; real Italian marble, and the finest selections of Mexican onyx, and but little of other materials is employed in its structure. This is equally true of the other two hotels.

In one, "The Cordova," is the famous sun-parlor, a room made entirely of glass and luxuriously furnished, where invalids may enjoy all the vivifying effects of sunlight, without being exposed to the lightest touch of outside air. In the other, "The Alcazar," are the same Moorish designs and furnishings, but he finds here an in-door swimming pool. It is deep and wide, and through it runs a stream of pure warm water. It is warm enough for the most delicate invalid in the coldest January day. It is all under roof, and all most systematically and conveniently arranged for both sexes and all ages.

But the acme is reached when all three of this unequaled group is seen at night, ablaze from roof to base with thousands of electric lights. It is worth coming far to see.

There need be no fear of promising too much when urging a traveler to visit St. Augustine. Words cannot tell one half its quaint beauty, the charm of its graceful age, nor the magnificence of its renewed youth.

The wonderful climate and the warm sea air of the Atlantic ocean, old Spanish landmarks, romantic scenery, marvelous treasures of architectural beauty and hotel accommodations of the highest grade, render it the equal of any winter watering-place on earth.

Year after year the attractions of St. Augustine have drawn increased numbers of pleasure seekers and invalids, until now it is the winter home of thousands.

In visiting St. Augustine one can scarcely go astray for a hotel. Of the celebrated Flagler group, the Ponce

Corners in St. Augustine.

de Leon accommodates 500 guests. Its charges are $5 per day and upwards. It is to be, this year, under the skillful management of Messrs. Gillis & Murray. The Alcazar which affords room for 300 is under the care of Joseph P. Greaves. Rates from $4.00 to $3.00. The Cordova is the annex which relieves the plethora of the other two.

Of other hotels there is a great abundance of all sorts and sizes, and in almost every street. A tabulated list will be found elsewhere. The largest and best, exclusive of the Flager hotels, is the San Marco, a short distance outside the city gates. It has a capacity of 500 with rates from $2.50 to $5.00 per day. Blanchard and Hager, Props.

To those who wish quiet elegance it is easy to recommend the Valencia, situated on St. George street south of the Plaza. It was constructed by the builders of the Ponce de Leon, and embodies the most perfect hotel arrangements of the day. All is homelike and comfortable within, and the broad verandas overlook spacious grounds filled with verdure and bloom.

It is conducted by Mrs. Frazer, a woman of fifteen years success in hotel management. This hotel can accommodate 100 guests. Rates $3.00 per day or $13.00 to $17.50 per week.

Another cosy, family hotel, on a quiet street, but re-

CRADDOCK HOUSE.
ST. AUGUSTINE, FLA.

This well known and popular house is now open for the season of 1855-6. It is within five minute walk of Post Office, Plaza and Bay.

TERMS EASY.

SPECIAL RATES BY THE WEEK, MONTH OR SEASON.

MRS. J. E. CRADDOCK.

moved only two blocks from the very heart of the city is the Craddock House on Bridge street.

It is admirably conducted by Mrs. J. E. Craddock, and is a favorite and popular house. Its capacity is 25; its terms are $1.50 to $2.00 per day with special rates by the week, month or season, or to families.

The following is a partial list of the other and smaller hotels, some of which may be found in almost every street.

LOCATION	NAME	CAPACITY	RATE PER DAY	PROPRIETOR
Facing the Bay	Ocean View	60 to 75	$2.00	W. S. M. Pinkham
St. George st.	Lorilard Vila	35	$2.00 to $3.00	Mrs. Hernandez
Faces the Plaza	Plaza Hotel	100	$2.00	S. F. Bennett
St. George st.	Magnolia	250	$3.00 to $4.00	
St. George st.	Palmetto	30	$2.00	J. S. Bentley
St. George st.	Columbia	50	$2.00	W. M. Teahen
Faces the Plaza	Algonquin	70	$2.00	G. S. Messerve

For those whose time is limited, an easy way to procure a fair idea of the beauties of St. Augustine is to leave Jacksonville on an early morning train, and arrive in St. Augustine before the middle of the forenoon. Go at once to the Ponce de Leon and register for lunch which is served from 1 to 3 p. m., and for which he will be charged $1.00. This makes the traveler a guest of the hotel, and at liberty to stroll through and examine its wonderful interior. He may also visit and explore the annexes, the Cordova and Alcazar. When lunch is served he may thus be admitted to the dining room—an art gallery in itself—and worth much more than the elaborate and princely meal which will be served beneath the stately dome.

If the lunch be partaken as soon as the room is open there will be time after it for a drive through the city to the plaza, the slave market, the cathedral, the old city gates, and the fort, and a return to the depot in time for the last train to Jacksonville. The train arrives at the latter place in time for a late dinner.

This way of seeing St. Augustine is simply reading the head lines, but it is better than missing it entirely.

To the Tourist.

Those who can proceed more leisurely will find that it will take many days to exhaust St. Augustine. It has many odd, half-hidden nooks, that it is a delight to explore.

For instance, walking towards the sea on the southern side of the Alameda, pass the northern end of the Cordova, and continue the stroll to the first corner occupied by a drug store. Turn this corner, and face southward keeping the right hand wall. After walking less than half a block, a wall presents itself that may easily be taken for the rear of some large building. Presently, it is possible, the seeker finds a closed (or open) door. If closed, and he dares pull the bell knob, and thus gain admission; or, if open, and he gratifies his curiosity by peeping in, he finds himself facing the end of a porch. It is on a level with the street, has a stone floor, is supported by stone columns, long and low, and runs at right angles with the street, and is really the front entrance of a dwelling-house. In a distance of not more than 100 feet he has passed from the busy, bustling crowds that throng the latest, most up-to-date structures, to the typical old St. Augustine of three centuries ago. The chances are that the wall through which the door admits him, and the floor he treads upon were put in place three hundred years before he was born, long before Mary, Queen of Scots, was beheaded, or Richelieu plotted. After thoroughly reconnoitering the city there are many

Pleasant Excursions

that may be made to points in the vicinity. The trip to Anastasia Island and Light House, is one of interest and easily made. To the North Beach is another trip full of delight.

For the philanthropist a place full of interest is the State asylum for the deaf, dumb, and blind. This is a flourishing institution under the charge of Prof. H. N. Felkel, and a corps of able assistants. Visitors are always welcome, and will find much to gratify and interest them. Take a carriage drive out through the city gates for more than half a mile beyond, then turn to the east or right and follow a pleasant road through the woods, till you come to the buildings in a cool, shady dell.

Four miles from St. Augustine, at a little place called Moultrie is the Carmona Vineyard, where there are seventy-five acres of grapes, and in the vicinity nearly 200 acres. This vineyard was set with White Niagaras in March, and shipments of grapes were made in June of the year following. The second year the yield was two and one-half tons to the acre.

To the Invalid.

It is hardly necessary to offer a guide to drug-stores, physicians or livery stables. The life of the city is along the Alameda, on the Plaza, and along St. George street, all within a stone's throw of each other, and drug stores and physicians' offices are interspersed at easy intervals and are unmistakable.

The liveries do not need to be sought. Jehus in stylish turnouts line the curbings and are ever alert, and come eagerly at the slightest beckoning.

To the Settler or Investor.

Any information regarding lands or real estate in or around St. Augustine, may be obtained by application to Mr. J. H. Slater. He not only is well and thoroughly informed, but may be implicitly trusted with business. He furnishes abstracts of property, and makes a specialty of exchanging northern for southern property. He may be found near the Cordova, in the heart of the city.

Palatka.

Distant from Jacksonville 56 miles. Fare $2.00. Take J., T. & K. W. R'y. or by the East Coast Line, which makes connection at this point with the G., S. & F. R. R., the J., T. & K. W. R'y., the Florida Southern Railway, and the St. John's River and Ocklawaha River steamboats.

Palatka has a population of about 6,000, and possesses all the conveniences of a modern town.

The hotels that are sure to be open the coming winter are the following:

PROPRIETOR		CAPACITY	RATE PER DAY	PER WEEK
S. Graham	Graham House	250	$2.50 to $3.00	$10 to $15
Jas. Gamble	St. George	100	$2.00 to $2.50	Special
J. Falk	Arlington	60	$2.00	

Continuing southward, the road veers to the east, and the water scenery changes from the St. John's to the Atlantic coast. Lift hats to the St. John's before leaving it, for it is a noble stream and worthy, and you have reached, at Palatka, the head of tide water navigation.

Ormond.

Distance from Jacksonville 65 miles. Fare $4.25. Take East Coast Line.

The first of the east coast towns is Ormond-on-the-Halifax. It is situated on both sides the Halifax river, the two portions of the town being connected by a bridge. Near the city, the Tomoka River, one of the most picturesque and interesting streams in all Florida joins the Halifax. This stream is easily explored by steam or naptha launches, or by sail or row boats, and the silvery Ormond Beach, four hundred feet wide, hard and level as an asphalt pavement, and extending thirty miles without a break, are the great attractions at this place. Here are also pleasant drives through fragrant pine woods, varied with groves of oak and palmetto. The surf-bathing is here superb, and may be indulged in five days out of seven throughout the winter season. Fishing here is unrivalled sport.

The Hotel Ormond is one of the finest and most complete in the State. It accommodates 275 guests; Rates $4.00 to $5.00 per day. The Coquina, Sunnyside and Granada are smaller, with capacities not above 70, and rates from $1.50 to $3.00 per day.

Daytona.

A sea-side town 110 miles from Jacksonville. Fare from Jacksonville $4.50.

Large numbers of northern families congregate yearly. Here are the winter cottages of several wealthy families whose homes would do credit to Cape May or Newport. They have their winter gardens, and their mid-winter roses, and are protected from the rougher Atlantic winds by a long wind-break of tall oleanders, that are themselves almost perpetual bloomers.

Small hotels and comfortable boarding houses abound, and are run at reasonable rates. The beautiful beach, fine drives, and excellent fishing are the attractions.

New Smyrna.

On the Atlantic coast 125 miles from Jacksonville. Fare from Jacksonville $5.10.

It is believed to be the oldest settlement in Florida, south of St. Augustine. It has the same fine beach, good fishing and boating, and an additional attraction in the ruins of an old sugar mill, built, it is supposed, more than one hundred years ago, by Turnbull, the indigo planter. Or, as some believe, it is the remains of a chapel built by

the followers of Columbus in 1496 or 1497. It is a puzzle to antiquarians, and is visited by scores of tourists yearly.

The three last mentioned points are favorite summer resorts for families from the interior portions of the peninsula. They come in great numbers to enjoy the surf-bathing, sea breeze and fish-diet.

Not far below this point, the road skirts the Indian River, and runs for many miles closely on its border. This famous body of water is not a river, not even a stream. It is simply an arm of the sea, shut in by sand dunes, and connected with the ocean by inlets and outlets. It has neither source, mouth nor current, but it swarms with fish, oyster beds, and water fowl, and all along its banks (or shores) is a country full of game, both large and small. The ride along this river is with the water and its saline breezes on the one side, and much of the way, an unbroken hammock wilderness on the other.

The first point of importance is

Titusville.

Distance from Jacksonville 160 miles. Fare from Jacksonville $5.60. Take either East Coast Line, or the J., T. & K. W. R'y., better known as The Tropical Trunk Line.

At Titusville the river is at its greatest width—six miles across. The town is the county seat of Brevard county, has electric lights, water works, etc, and many important industries, that of shipping fresh fish in ice being a lucrative and rapidly growing one. Two live weekly newspapers keep Titusville and Brevard county conspicuously before the world.

The hotels are

NAME	CAPACITY	RATES PER DAY	PROPRIETOR
Indian River Hotel	200	$3.00	O. H. Voss
Lund House	50	$1.50	W. Lund

Here, as elsewhere, are small boarding houses, for local accommodation chiefly, but sometimes admit a few winter visitors.

Throughout this country, the traveler is in the very home of the celebrated Indian River oranges. Hidden away back among the deeps of the hammocks of which he sees but the outer green walls, and fringe of tall palmetto trees, are groves wide in extent, and mammoth in the proportions of their trees. This year, however, the trees are simply stately, ghostly skeletons. Nothing could more fully illustrate the wondrous fertility of the soil, or the recuperative qualities of the climate than these groves, as seen in the closing summer and early autum. Green sprouts from the roots, and vigorous shoots from the trunk have in the past few months stretched upward until, in many cases, their lusty growth is seen protruding through and above the boughs of the old tree. From Titusville, the cry is "On to Palm Beach!" Indeed, the fever to move rapidly to this objective point is felt immediately upon leaving St. Augustine.

South of Titusville the journey may be continued by water or by rail. By water, by taking the steamer of the Indian River Steamboat Co.; by rail, by the East Coast Line. As the flourishing little towns along the river are built immediately on the bank, they are in full view from the river. As each was until this year embowered in its orange groves, and a continuous line of groves filled the intervening spaces of country, the ride on the river, was one long to be remembered.

On leaving Titusville the railroad departs from the river and running back of the towns, the traveler in some instances only knows of their proximity, by reading their names on the little stations, where a carriage is waiting to convey him riverward to the town.

Such a place is City Point; another is Rockledge, in previous seasons known far and wide for its fine hotel, the Hotel Indian River. It is doubtful if this hotel will be

open during the coming winter, not because Rockledge is less delightful than ever, but because of business complications.

Other energetic, thriving river towns are Sharpe's, Eau Gallie, Melbourne, and Cocoa, all possessing unrivalled opportunities for fishing, boating and hunting.

On to Palm Beach.

Leaving these, and hastening onward, and southward, still hugging the river bank more or less closely; the scenery changes. All traces of orange trees, dead or alive, disappear. Pineapple patches appear, in regular set rows. They increase as the train speeds on until the patches blend into fields and the fields coalesce, until at last the run is through from eighteen to twenty-five miles or more of almost continuous pineapple fields. Nor are these narrow strips beside the railroad, but they stretch out on either side as far as the eye can reach. They seem like the great corn or wheat fields of the northwest, or the endless cotton plantations of the lower Mississippi valley.

The country becomes hilly, and still the spiny rows are not interrupted, they climb hills and pass over them to the other side, ascending and descending slopes and traversing valleys or covering levels with the same precision.

Just as this profusion begins to decline again into interrupted patches West Palm Beach is announced.

Lake Worth.

Distance from Jacksonville 300 miles. Fare from Jacksonville $11.40.

The reader need not fear to betray his ignorance by asking: "What is Lake Worth?" because Lake Worth is a recent discovery. For a score of years a few early pioneers, whose thrilling experiences with wildcats, panthers, rattlesnakes and alligators would fill volumes, lived a somewhat lonely, but really blissful, life amid the surpassing beauties of Lake Worth. Near Jupiter Lighthouse Indian River returns to the sea which gave it, and, as a river, terminates its existence. Eight miles south of this point, and nearly 300 miles south of Jacksonville, lies Lake Worth. It is a long, narrow sheet of water running parallel with the ocean. Like the Indian River, its name is a misnomer. It is a body of salt water connected with the ocean by inlets. Like all the waters of Florida it is a clear amber color, its bottom easily visible anywhere. It is many miles long, and is at most places less than a mile or a half mile in width. Houses on either shore are plainly visible from the other. It is separated from the ocean by a narrow strip of land. Along its shores all tropical growths are perfectly at home. Huge rubber trees flourish as if in Brazilian forests. The orange has never thriven here, but this is the region of the cocoanut and the pineapple, and all other fully tropical fruits.

Struggling settlers dotted its shores with their homes, and until the last three or four years lived in almost utter isolation. Then by some happy chance, this genuine paradise was discovered by enterprise, capital and good taste. Along its shores little towns have sprung up and flourished like gourd vines.

Lake Worth may be reached by two routes—the Jacksonville, Tampa and Key West Railway to Titusville, thence by Indian River Steamboat Company to Jupiter, thence by Jacksonville and Lake Worth Railway to Juno near the head of Lake Worth. The other route is entirely by rail from Jacksonville to West Palm Beach direct via the East Coast Line.

West Palm Beach.

This is the metropolis of Lake Worth and the present terminus of the East Coast Line. It has sprung within the

Glimpses of the Coast.

E. H. DIMICK, Prop.   LEE RUSSELL, M'gr.

WEST PALM BEACH DRUG STORE

DEALERS IN

Drugs, Toilet Articles, Druggists' Sundries,

FINE STATIONERY AND SCHOOL BOOKS.

PRESCRIPTIONS CAREFULLY COMPOUNDED.

WEST PALM BEACH,   -   -   FLORIDA.

O. W. WEYBRECHT,
DEALER IN HARDWARE.

Plumber, Steam and Gas Fitter. Tin, Copper and Iron Work.

DEALER IN

Pumps, Fittings and General Plumbing Supplies, Tinware, Agate Ware, and House Furnishings of Every Kind.
Agent for the Aermotor.   Constructor of Irrigation Plants.
Estimates for Work and Material.

One or Both Promptly Furnished.

WEST PALM BEACH,   -   -   -   FLORIDA.

A. D. 1865.   A. D. 1895.

W. C. C. Branning,

West Palm Beach,

Florida.

Fine Watch and Jewelry Repairer.
Thirty Years' Practical Experience.

short space of two years from a pineapple plantation to a town of nearly 1,000 inhabitants. It has paved streets, a fine water-works system, a bank, two newspapers, etc., and bids fair to be within a few years one of the most attractive towns in Florida. Many businesses are already established, and in dimensions that would do credit to a town of 20,000. The town has all the push and bustle and much of the crudeness of the mushroom towns of the early West. Every want of the tourist or settler can be supplied at the stores in this little town.

The invalid will find at the store of Mr. E. H. Dimick a full assortment of pure, fresh drugs, fine stationery, all kinds of toilet articles, and other goods usually found in a first-class city drug store. Mr. Dimick has been president of the Lake Worth Preserving Company, which makes a specialty of the manufacture of guava jelly.

The tourist who is fond of outdoor sports can find no better place in which to enjoy either fishing, boating or hunting, for either large or small game. Full equipments for either angler or hunter can be obtained at the very complete hardware store of O. W. Weybrecht, on Clematis avenue, in almost the center of the town, and nearly opposity the city bank.

The curio hunter will find much that is unique in this locality, at the watch-repairing establishment of Mr. W. C. C. Branning, near Weybrecht's store. Mr. Branning not only repairs jewelry with a skill that comes from thirty years' experience, but is an artist in alligator ivory. He carves in high relief on alligator teeth or wild boar tusks a deer hunt with hounds in full cry, or pointers at a stand, or retrieve, in the most spirited and life-like attitudes, and with the highest finish.

There is also at West Palm Beach a dealer in bird plumes. The beautiful, large white cranes and snowy egrets, which a few years ago were seen in immense flocks, often in thousands, on every river and lake in Florida, are now seldom seen. They are, in fact, practically extinct, except that in the deep recesses of the Everglades they are still found in considerable quantities. During the month of April, when the plumage is most beautiful, the Indians emerge from the Everglades and appear in this little town loaded with the plumes. This local dealer buys them and ships to a firm in Jacksonville, whence they are again shipped to New York. The books of this dealer show that his purchases, day after day during the season, foot up from $60 to $110 worth per day. When it is remembered that the superb bird, found nowhere else on the continent, is killed to procure often less than a dozen delicate fringe-like feathers that grow on the upper part of the back, and which are as light as thistle-down, and the fact that some of the Indians bring in a pound or more each day, it is easy to estimate the immense slaughter. Moreover, it is during the nesting season that the plumage is most beautiful, and every bird killed leaves a brood of little ones to perish. Extermination is not far off. The plumes at Palm Beach brings $7.00 per ounce. The more dainty egrets are sometimes rated at $35.00 per ounce. The State Legislature has endeavored more than once to prohibit this slaughter by law, but, as history proves, the Seminole has never come under the laws of the white man. No law reaches or troubles the Florida Indian. The reform must come from the other end of the line. The "coming woman," of whom we have such nauseating doses nowadays, has developed a good deal of force. If this could be exerted in a good direction, and declare these plumes unfashionable, the traffic would soon cease. As long as the demand continues, the Indian will procure his whisky and ammunition by this convenient means until the supply is exhausted.

If the traveler arrives before "the season" is fully opened he looks in vain for a hotel, while right before his face is the most celebrated all-the-year-house on the whole length of the coast—Vail's Floating Hotel.

Stepping from the train, the traveler is met by a polite porter who takes his grip, and with a wave of the hand

and "dis way, sah," guides across a track to a plank walk, and with two or three steps he is in the forward end of a steamboat, and he is asked to register, for it is also a cosy little hotel office.

When the rush for the lower Indian River began, the only inhabitants anywhere near Jupiter Inlet was the family of the light-house keeper. Captain Vail took the steamer Rockledge from the upper Indian River, remodeled it and anchored it at the inlet for the accommodation of the on-coming prospectors. It here did capital service as a hotel for four years. When the cry came, "Onward to West Palm Beach!" he pulled up his anchor and put his hotel in motion. He entered Lake Worth and cast anchor snugly beside the railroad and depot.

The East Coat Line is rapidly extending still southward to Biscayne Bay as a terminus. As the season opens the Floating Hotel will follow the tide of travel. It will be found during the early winter at New River, and later at Biscayne Bay, where it will do its part for the comfort of the public until the contemplated hotel at Biscayne Bay is completed. It will accommodate 60 guests; its rates are $3.00 per day.

Another hotel at West Palm Beach is Park Cottage; faces the lake at the foot of the city wharf; has a capacity of 25; rates $2.00 to $3.00 per day. Proprietor, O. Howes. Open in winter only.

In the scarcity of hotels, a cosy and comfortable recourse is in rented furnished rooms, in which one may become quite at home, and with very little trouble practice what is called light housekeeping. The Branning Bakery on Clematis avenue, or John Seybold on Narcissus street, can furnish all kinds of breads, cakes, pies, etc., made fresh every day, at reasonable prices. All kinds of fresh groceries and meats are easily procured. This mode of passing a winter is found to be both economical and homelike, and for invalids more quiet than life in a hotel.

The great feature and attraction of this locality is not

at West Palm Beach, but across the lake at Palm Beach proper. This is the

Hotel Royal Poinciana.

The lake at this point is 1,300 feet wide, and on the opposite side, in full view from every part of West Palm Beach, is the imposing front of the Royal Poinciana. It might well be called a royal structure from its appearance, but it receives its name from the *royal poinciana*, a tree of wondrous beauty and tropic bloom which grows in rich abundance in the grounds.

The building was erected in 1894 by Mr. H. M. Flagler, and is a splendid structure in the colonial style of architecture. It is six stories high, and from the tower which crowns its roof a most magnificent view may be had of

ocean, lake, canal, river and forest scenery, an area of nearly twenty miles north and south. It is 700 feet long, and will shelter in an emergency 1,000 guests. It has an elegant ball-room, an immense and finely decorated dining-room, a commodious colonial sitting-room and tasteful parlors. It faces the west, on the lake, while in the rear, only about a quarter of a mile, is its attachment or annex, the Beach Pavilion. Here are numerous guests' rooms, a superb cafe, swimming pools, supplied with sulphur and ocean water—warm or cold—baths and bath-houses. Surf-bathing may be indulged in every day in the year.

The popularity of this hotel during the season of 1894–95 was phenomenal. For weeks it was necessary to give unfavorable replies to hundreds of applicants for rooms. For the purpose of providing ample hotel accommodations in the future, the Palm Beach Inn (by the sea) is now being built, and will be open for the season of 1895-96. It is a fine building, containing 400 guest chambers and all the accessories of a modern first-class hotel. It faces the ocean, and from its spacious varandas the views are superb. A pier 1,000 feet in length is in course of construction, to be run straight out into the ocean in front of this Inn-by-the-Sea.

To reach Palm Beach and the Royal Poinciana take the ferry at the end of the city wharf a few hundred feet from the depot.

The rates are $5.00 per day and upward. It will this winter be under the management of Mr. Henry W. Merrill.

The Inn-by-the-Sea will be finished by the opening of

JOHN SEYBOLD,
BAKERY & CONFECTIONERY,

Narcissus St. - - WEST PALM BEACH.

the season, and will be in charge of Mr. C. Davis. Its rates will be $4.00 per day and upwards.

There is no way at present of going further south than Lake Worth except by stage and sailboat. But this will not be the case for long. The East Coast Line is to be immediately extended to Biscayne Bay. Another of the mammoth Flagler hotels will be erected at its terminus. So eager is the rush to this point, that wild, uncleared land is already held at the fabulous price of $1,000 per acre. At present there are no accommodations for travelers south of Lake Worth other than tenting out.

Turning northward, steps must be retraced to Titusville, from which point the J., T. & K. W. R'y may be taken to

Sanford.

Distance from Jacksonville 125 miles. Fare $3.75. Take J., T. & K. W. at Union Depot.

This is a pleasant city on Lake Monroe. It has perhaps 1,000 or 1,200 inhabitants, and is a well-kept, attractive city.

The principal hotel which will be open this winter is the Wilton House, capable of taking care of 35 guests. Its rates are $2.00 to $3.00 per day. A. Rogers, proprietor. Other smaller houses are Comfort Cottage, Sirrene House

RHOADS & CO.,
..... DRUGGISTS

PICO BLOCK,
SANFORD, FLA.

THE HOTEL WILTON,
SANFORD, FLORIDA.

Elegantly Furnished.
    Electric Service.
        Artesian Water.

Cor. Third St. and Magnolia Ave.
A. ROBBINS, - - - Proprietor.

and Mrs. Toler's boarding house, all of which, while depending chiefly upon local patronage, make way for a few tourists upon occasion. The best drug store is that of Rhoades & Co., in the Pico Block. Livery stables near depot.

DeLand.

Distance from Jacksonville 112 miles. Fare $3.75. Take J., T. & K. W.

This is an ideal winter residence city. It has the appearance of a prosperous Central New York town, which it greatly resembles. Before the destruction of the orange groves it was possibly the most attractive place in Florida. It was embowered, framed in and surrounded by orange groves of uncommon thrift and beauty. It is still a town of beautiful homes. It has paved streets, electric lights, fine business blocks, and all conveniences of express office, money order office, etc. It is the seat of the Stetson University, a flourishing institution for both sexes, where many Northern families place their children during the winter season.

There are pleasant excursions to be made from this place, of which that to DeLeon Springs is one of the most

J. F. ALLEN.   JAMES ALLEN.

J. F. ALLEN & CO.

DEALERS IN

Furniture. Sewing Machines. Wall Paper. Carpets
AND MATTINGS.

CITY UNDERTAKERS.

DELAND, - - - - - - FLORIDA.

CHANDLER ✶ HOUSE,

DeLAND, FLORIDA.

Next Door to the Court-House.
Newly Renovated and Refurnished.

NEW MANAGEMENT.

Terms, - - - $1.50 to $3 per Day.

Mrs. CARLISLE & SISTERS,

PROPRIETORS.

delightful. Good hunting for small game in all the surrounding country.

The hotels here are much above those usually found at inland towns. They rank with the best in the State. They are:

NAME.	CAPACITY.	RATES PER DAY.	PROPRIETOR.
College Arms	75	$3.50	G. W. Ripley
Putnam House	150	$2.50 to $3.00	M. E. Gould
Carrolton	75	$2.00 to $2.50	G. A. Drake
Chandler	20	$1.50 to $2.00	Mrs. Carlisle
Floral Grove	24	$2.00	J. C. Baird
Waverly House	20	$8.00 per week	Mrs. Drake

Of these the Putnam House is in the midst of its own orange grove—a grove which is so rapidly putting forth after its freezing that it will be quite itself again in a few years. The management aims to conduct this house in such a manner that the transient tourists will go away with pleasant recollections, and the permanent guests will have a happy, healthful, jovial winter in Florida's genial clime.

The Chandler House, situated in the very center of the town, next the court house and opposite the Volusia County Bank, has not, of late years, enjoyed the highest reputation. But, in anticipation of the winter's travel, the house has been leased to new parties, and has been thoroughly renovated, and under the able charge of Mrs. Carlisle and sisters, has become the favorite house with those discriminating judges, the drummers, for whom it is admirably situated.

Besides the hotels there are houses that offer rooms, furnished or unfurnished, at reasonable rates. Those who wish the former will find a pleasant place in the very center of the town where meals and lunches will be served them at all hours. This is the Home Restaurant, formerly the Royal Cafe. It is conducted by Mesdames Tiffany and Hale, who thoroughly know their business.

Those who prefer the unfurnished rooms will find at the establishment of J. F. Allen & Co. a large and complete assortment of everything needed for comfort or elegance, any of which may be rented for use during the season at reasonable rates. (See card.)

Gainesville.

Distance from Jacksonville 71 miles. Fare $2.80. Take the J., T. & K. W. via Palatka, or F. C. & P. direct.

Gainesville, the county seat of Alachua county, is situated almost geographically in the center of the State, and is one of the healthiest and most attractive cities of Florida. It is noted for its beautifully paved streets and good roads. The population numbers about 5,000, and fluctuates but little, as it depends very slightly upon winter travel, owing to its lack of large hotels. A disastrous fire, which occurred in 1889, destroyed two of the largest, which have never been rebuilt, but several small but comfortable hotels and numerous boarding houses supply accommodations for the tourist or transient visitor.

Its school advantages are among the best. The East Florida Seminary and Military School has its home here, and a fine graded and high school offers an excellent free education to all. Several prosperous private schools are here conducted. Most of the various religious denominations have elegant and commodious edifices, and the clergy are renowned for their eloquence and zeal. The citizens are hospitable and cultured, and are about equally composed of Northerners and Southerners. New comers are welcomed, and find among the various churches and societies many social pleasures. A good opera house under capable management affords amusements of diverse character and suited to all tastes.

Occupying an altitude of 173 feet above sea level and remote from water courses, the climate is remarkably salubrious, and has a mean temperature of 73°.

HOTEL PUTNAM

DeLAND, FLORIDA.

To those who have been guests of this Hotel we wish to announce that the house is again open and in better shape than ever to take care of its winter visitors. We earnestly hope that our former patrons will be with us again during the coming winter, and promise to do all in our power to make the season as pleasant as have been those in the past.

It is situated in the midst of a bearing orange grove, the fruit of which is entirely at the disposal of the guests. The house is well furnished has, and all the appointments of a first-class hotel. Everything is arranged to secure the comfort of its guests, and the management promises to conduct it in such a manner that the transient tourists will go away with pleasant recollections and the permanent guests will have a happy, healthful, jovial winter in Florida's genial clime.

M. E. GOULD, Prop'r.

⇾HOME RESTAURANT.⇽

DeLAND, FLORIDA.

Mesdames TIFFANY & HALE.

BAKERY ᴬᴺᴅ LUNCHES.

SODA WATER AND CIGARS.

⇾ HOME COOKING. ⇽

J. G. Nichols.   H. F. Dutton.   W. G. Robinson.

H. F. DUTTON & CO.,

BANKERS,

AND DEALERS IN

SEA ISLAND COTTON,

GAINESVILLE, FLORIDA.

FOREIGN AGENCIES:
Liverpool and Manchester, Eng.
Alexandria, Egypt.

H. G. ROBINSON,
323 Broad Street,
PROVIDENCE, R. I.

J. W. MARSH,

DRY GOODS and SHOES.

GAINESVILLE, FLORIDA.

Mosquitoes are almost unknown, and no objectionable features of insect life are met with.

The city is lighted with gas, and has an abundant supply of spring water, which an analysis made in Washington, D. C., shows to be almost chemically pure. Consequently the health of the city is remarkably good. Many pleasant resorts are within easy distance over good roads, and excellent teams are always to be had at reasonable rates. Oliver Park, two and one-ha'f miles distant, is nicely fitted up for picnic parties, with walks, pavilion, bowling alley, swings, etc. The Sink, or Payne's Prairie, and Newnan's Lake are each about three and five miles away, and offer good fishing and boating. The Devil's Mill Hopper is about six miles, and is a natural depression of nearly 100 feet, with a circumference at the top of about the same diameter, narrowing sharply to a small lake at the bottom, fed by innumerable little springs which trickle down its sides amidst luxuriant tropical foliage of vines and plants. One charm in visiting it to the young couples, with whom it is a favorite resort, is that it is almost impossible to reach it without getting lost among the numerous circuitous routes, and that excuse is considered a legitimate reason for a too prolonged stay. "Warren's Cave" is another great natural curiosity about fifteen miles away, but easily reached. Descending a dry sink, the mouth of the cavern is entered about thirty feet down the side. It is about five feet at the entrance, gradually widening to seven, and descending until about thirty feet from the entrance it takes a sudden drop to the level of the bottom of the sink, some fifty feet. At the extreme end of this room or widening is a circular hole, a few inches in diameter, which lets the water out. From this room a gallery extends upward a number of feet. In this was found a stake projecting about two feet from the surface, having a ring worn just below the extended top, as if by a chain. Near this was found a skull and other human bones, now in the possession of the Museum. Numerous galleries leading off have not been explored owing to their narrowness. The whole cavern is lined with a wall of limestone, and is evidently a natural formation, but that it has been used by human beings at some period is shown by the stake and bones.

Various other attractive excursions can be made to points of interest, and during the entire year the different railroads offer extremely low rates to excursionists to all interesting parts of the State.

Gainesville is comfortably reached from all portions of Florida, and the traveler is met by hacks at all trains.

FURNISHED ROOMS
FOR RENT.

MRS. L. A. THRASHER,
Cor. East Main and Mechanic Sts.,

⁂ Gainesville, Florida.

BOOKS AND STATIONERY.

JAMES BELL,
East Side Public Square,
Opp. Court House.

GAINESVILLE, FLA.

NATIONAL AND STATE PAPERS,
LEADING PERIODICALS, NOVELS,
DIARIES, SCHOOL BOOKS, BASE BALL GOODS
Etc., Etc., Etc.

At Gainesville is the principal market for the Sea Island cotton of the State. It is handled entirely by the firm of H. F. Dutton & Co., who ship it direct to Europe. This firm conducts a very heavy business besides in Sea Island cotton seed, bagging, cotton seed fertilizer, ginning supplies, etc., adding much to the life and prosperity of the town.

There are many large dry goods and other stores. J. W. Marsh, a dealer in dry goods and shoes, will be found on the square, facing the court house. His house is quite complete.

The best hotel is the Brown House, which has a capacity of 75 at $2.50 per day. B. S. Starke, proprietor.

Giddings & Co. are leading druggists.

J. O. Andrews, real estate dealer and secretary of the Board of Trade, is the proper person to whom to apply for information regarding lands, phosphate and business openings. He is thoroughly informed and thoroughly reliable.

Fine livery stables are run by W. R. Thomas and by W. H. Davis & Co.

Dr. N. D. Phillips. Dr. Lancaster and the Drs. McInstry are any of them skillful physicians of good standing.

Those wishing reading matter, fine stationery, or other supplies, will find all they can ask at the store of Judge James Bell, facing the court house on the square. He has the New York daily papers, all the standard periodicals and current literature, as well as a fine supply of the latest books and popular literature.

Those desiring more quiet or a little more independence than that offered in hotel life may find nicely furnished rooms at Mrs. Thrasher's, on the corner of East Maine and Mechanic streets.

✦ OCALA ✦

IF YOU WANT

Timber Lands,
or Phosphate Lands,
or Farm Lands,
or Vegetable Lands,

OR ANY KIND OF FLORIDA PROPERTY,

CALL ON OR ADDRESS,

J. H. LIVINGSTON & SONS.
Room 9, Marion Block.

W. H. MAREAN, M. D.,
Homeopathic Physician and Surgeon.

Thirty Years' Practice.
Twelve Years' Experience with
Diseases Incident to Florida.

CHRONIC DISEASES — ✦

Successfully treated by mail.

Address Lock Box 514,

OCALA, FLORIDA.

Ocala.

Distance from Jacksonville 101 miles. Fare $3.90. Take F. C. & P. or J., T. & K. W. at Union Depot.

Ocala, known as the Brick City, is situated in the center of the peninsula, and is the county seat of Marion county. It claims 6,000 inhabitants, and is a beautiful, live and progressive city, with all modern facilities and conveniences.

To an invalid seeking health in the gentle climate of Florida, and those whose condition, physically, forbids a residence near a water course or a sea coast, Ocala is to be especially recommended for its high altitude and general healthfulness.

For a business man desiring to engage in lucrative business or seeking a safe investment for his capital, this city stands second to none in the State for his purposes.

To a weary business man of the North who wishes to leave his business cares behind him and bask for a brief season 'neath Florida's sunny skies away from the rush and turmoil of larger cities, Ocala offers inducements peculiarly her own. Here, surrounded by a spirit of culture and refinement, he may rest in quiet contentment, and return home after his pleasant sojourn refreshed in mind and body, with larger views of humanity and less a slave to mammon, since he has witnessed how happy and contented are many of Ocala's inhabitants who live well and contented with very little money at their command.

No better place in the State can be found by those wishing to engage in agricultural pursuits than the immediate vicinity of Ocala. The soil is very productive, easily tilled, yielding abundant and diversified crops. All kinds of stock thrive splendidly, as well as poultry of every description. The price of land is reasonable, and a ready market is found in Ocala for every kind of country produce.

This is the center of the phosphate industry, phosphate

THE
Montezuma Hotel,

MRS. KATE C. BATTY,
    Proprietress.

Ocala, Florida.

OPEN THE YEAR ROUND.

Rates $2 to $2.50 per day.
Special rates by the week.

FREE SAMPLE ROOM
For Convenience of Commercial Travelers.

---

in large abundance having been discovered in this county a few years since. This industry alone is an immense source of wealth to Marion county, which annually exports thousands of tons of this wonderful commodity.

A plan which bids fair to be realized is in view to erect and equip an immense fertilizer factory, with a promised capital of $200,000. This plan is to be perfected at an early date to prepare the natural phosphate suitable for fertilizing purposes, and will increase the wealth of Ocala very materially.

Aside from the fertilizer factory, she has several other new enterprises in course of construction, embracing an electric street railway, having connection with Silver Springs, which will be completed in time for the convenience of the winter tourists. A new brewery, an ice factory and a telephone exchange are nearing completion.

This enterprising and bustling city is situated 100 miles directly south of Jacksonville, being midway between that city and Tampa. It is but six miles from the beautiful, far-famed and picturesque Silver Springs, with its natural wells, sub-marine forest, ever-changing hued waters, and other wonderful attractions, the beauty of which are indescribable. It is only twenty miles from the hunter's and angler's paradise, Homosassa and Crystal River.

There are three railroads entering the city limits, viz.: The Florida Central and Peninsular Railroad, the Silver Springs, Ocala and Gulf, and the Florida Southern Railways, which last is a portion of the Plant System.

The city has numerous restaurants and hotels. Among the latter will be found the Montezuma, which accommodates 100 guests; the Central Hotel, the Allred Hotel and the Arlington, all of which are under excellent management.

Among Ocala's other advantages are an accommodating bank, the Merchants' National, the Buffum Loan and Trust Company, building and loan associations, large steam and Chinese laundries, cigar factories, foundry and machine works, wagon and carriage factories, saw and planing mills, etc.

The dry goods, clothing and grocery stores are many, and have full and varied stocks, and it may be said with emphasis that nowhere in Florida can the necessaries of life be obtained at more reasonable rates than in this city.

The price of real estate in Ocala is also very reasonable. The most extensive dealer in this line is the agency of J. H. Livingston, who can be recommended for his honesty and fair dealing. This agency also handles phosphate and farming lands, and would doubtless be of great assistance to any one who may be interested in the genial and breezy climes of Florida.

Like all live and push-ahead cities, Ocala has a good share of newspapers, among them are the Ocala *Banner* the *Baptist Witness* and the *Marion Free Press*, all enjoying good circulations.

All religious denominations are represented in Ocala, with handsome structures for places of worship.

The city's educational advantages are unsurpassed. It has an excellent system of public schools, a graded high school, a female seminary and a kindergarten, besides several private schools. A business college under competent management has also recently been established.

The public library, comprising three thousand volumes of standard works, is an honor to the city and to the State as well. In this connection it might be well to mention that Ocala is the most noted literary center in the State, being the home of Mrs. Beatrice Marean, dramatist, and author of "The Tragedies of Oak Hurst," and many other works, whose reputation is national. Ocala is also the residence of Mrs. General J. A. Dickison, author of "Dickison and His Men." Besides these distinguished authors there are quite a number of other writers who wield facile and interesting pens.

The Public Library and Debating Society compose a large membership, and is a source of benefit to its members and the public. This association, as well as the Choral Society and Metropolitan Brass Band are truly worthy of a larger city.

For Ocala's protection she is proud to mention the names of the Ocala Rifles and the Ocala Fire Department. For their respective duties they are well equipped and well drilled. Hose Company No. 4 of the fire department at present holds the championship of the State

The social element of Ocala is first-class in every particular, there being such an excellent distinction of classes as is not often witnessed in a city of its size.

Both the legal and medical professions are well represented. Among the latter Ocala has numerous allopathic and one homeopathic physician, Dr. Wm. H. Marean, one of the most prominent and widely-read physicians in the South.

Marti City, the pretty little suburb of Ocala, with a population of 500 people, is composed of the best class of Cubans. The inhabitants of this village are engaged in the manufacture of cigars and cigarettes. Among the largest manufactories, of which there are ten, will be found those of Jose Morales & Co. and J. De la Cuesta, whose yearly outputs are immense.

It was near Ocala that the first discovery of phosphate in Florida was made. In the digging of a well suspicious-looking material was brought to the surface. It was analyzed, brought to the attention of capitalists, and in three months the ten acres around the well had sold for $68,000. This was the beginning of the now famous Dunnellon mine. Another owner of a piece of land for which he had paid $4,000 sold out for $30,000. A farmer starving on a half-cleared homestead remote from market sold out for $25,000. A real estate dealer in Jacksonville caught whispers of what was for some time carefully guarded as a secret, plunged boldly in. He cleared a quarter of a million in three weeks.

To see and find out all about mining of phosphate, visit Dunnellon, southwest from Ocala.

To see river or pebble phosphate, go to Peace River, near Arcadia, on the Jacksonville, Tampa and Key West R'y, 76 miles south of Bartow.

The whole subject of phosphate is one of wonderful interest to the geologist, investor or curious tourist.

Continuing the tour southward, many thriving little towns are passed, but the objective point is

Tampa.

Distance from Jacksonville 212 miles. Fare $8.00. Take F. C & P. R'y or J., T. & K. W. at Union Depot.

Population in 1894, 16,000; in 1895, 21,000.

On May 25, 1839, Fernando DeSoto sailed into Espiritu Santo (Tampa Bay) and landed at what is now known as Spanish Park, a place about two miles east of Tampa, on the bay.

About 1832 Indians began threatening the few scattered settlers in this vicinity.

In 1835 a government post was established here The settlers soon moved in under its protection.

Through the years of Indian hostilities, ranging almost continuously from 1835 to 1856, this section was one of much activity owing to the large number of troops stationed here. The government had a line of steamers running to New Orleans and another running to Ft. Myers.

In the fifties Colonel H. L. Hart established a stage line from here to Palatka and Jacksonville, the journey consuming six or seven days. The same is now made in as many hours. This service continued for about twenty years.

When the Florida Railway and Navigation Company, now the Florida Central and Peninsular Railway, was built to Cedar Keys, the trip to Jacksonville was made by steamer to Cedar Keys, thence by rail.

In 1884 the South Florida Railway was built into Tampa, and in the spring of 1885, through the efforts of Gavino Gutierrez, the place was brought to the notice of large cigar manufacturers who were contemplating opening branch houses in the South.

On September 26, 1885, Mr. V. M. Ybor came here prospecting, and was located way out in the woods, now the site of the prosperous Ybor City. The average weekly pay-roll of these factories is this year $65,000.

Tampa Bay Hotel was begun in 1888 and completed early in 1890, when it was opened.

In 1890 the Florida Central and Peninsular Railway was completed to this city

A large, commodious and splendidly-appointed court house, occupying an entire square, was erected in the center of the business portion of the city in 1892. All the county officers are located in it. In the city hall, just across the street on the south side, can be found the city clerk, police and fire department.

In the city there are three substantial banking institutions, the First National, Exchange National and the Citizens' Bank and Trust Company, all of which are located on Franklin, the principal street.

The churches of Tampa are: St. Andrews Episcopal Church; St. Louis (Catholic); Presbyterian; Southern Methodist; Congregational; Baptist; Lutheran; Seventh Day Adventist, and the Schaarai Zedek Congregational.

Convent of Mary Immaculate, Mother Superior Theophile. Located on Twigg street, three blocks east of Franklin street. All branches of scholarship are taught, music and languages.

Newspapers—*Tampa Daily Times*, a successor of the *Tribune*, established 1876, consolidated with the *Journal* established 1886; they publish a weekly edition. Office corner of Franklin and Washington streets.

Daily Tribune, established in March, 1892; was run as daily during winter and weekly during summer. It started as a daily last January, and has continued as such. They publish a weekly edition also,

Daily News, established March 15, 1887.

Board of Trade—John Trice, President; W. H. Pearson, Secretary. Chartered in February, 1895. They contemplate erecting an expensive building soon, opposite the court house.

Tampa Rifles—A military organization of forty-two members. Captain, Fred W. Krause.

BAKER ✣ SEMINARY.

Florida Avenue.
TAMPA, - - FLORIDA.
Boarding and Day School for Young Ladies
AND SMALL BOYS.

This School is centrally located in a pleasant part of the city. The course of instruction is complete and under the care of competent instructors.

The Principal, Mrs. Irene Pennington, has charge of the higher branches, History, Literature, Rhetoric, etc.

Miss Nellie Collin, Intermediate Department.
Miss Esther Wilson, Primary Grade Department.
Miss Bessie Mills, Kindergarten Department.
Rev. H. B. Sommerlan, native of Cuba, Spanish.
Mrs. Weller, Instrumental and Vocal Music.
Miss Lottie E. Watkins, Art Department, in which the course is complete.

FRENCH AND GERMAN ARE ALSO TAUGHT.

Terms in accordance with course of study pursued.
For further information apply to Principal.

MRS. IRENE PENNINGTON,
TAMPA, FLA.

FOR GOOD INVESTMENTS SEE
J. M. FERNANDEZ,
REAL ESTATE AND LOANS,
TAMPA, - - FLORIDA.

PALMETTO ✻ HOTEL,
TAMPA, FLORIDA.

R. F. WEBB, - - Proprietor.

Renovated and Refurnished.

TWO BLOCKS FROM SOUTH FLORIDA DEPOT.

Rates, - - $2.00 to $3.00 per Day.

Special Rates by the Week and to Families.

Largely owing to its fine location, and very much more owing to the far-sighted wisdom and business acumen of Mr. H. B. Plant, who early recognized the importance of the location, and again owing to the enterprise of her citizens who reached out inviting hands to capital and enterprise, Tampa is not only a hustling, bustling, wide-awake city, but a most attractive, picturesque town. It has fine brick blocks, and handsome homes, wide, well-paved streets, and when its extreme youth is considered, a surprisingly settled and well-established air.

From all parts of the city a conspicuous object in the landscape is an elegant mosque-like building, with silvery turrets and towers, each surmounted by a gilded crescent. It suggests the Orient and the Moslem. One almost expects to see a long-robed Mohammedan step out upon one of the tower balconies, and, with face to the east, call the faithful to prayer.

It is a very large and strikingly beautiful building, and stands quite out from the city, with no surroundings but its own extensive and magnificent grounds.

This is the famous

Tampa Bay Hotel.

This magnificent structure is situated across a small arm of the bay from the city, but in full view. It is reached from the city by a bridge, but trains stop at Tampa as at a station, and then continue around the city and draw up almost at the entrance to the hotels. Indeed, passengers alight at the gates entering the grounds. Here in midwinter they walk through choice shrubbery and beds of blooming calla lilies to the main entrance, where they pass through elaborately carved doors of solid mahogany into what might well be mistaken for an art gallery. They stand amid groups of statuary, and on either hand are paintings of priceless value. Above them is a circular gallery, which is a picture gallery, where hang gems of the world's great painters. Long halls, 700 feet in length, are

E. M. HENDRY.   A. J. KNIGHT.

HENDRY & KNIGHT,

Real Estate Dealers.   Investors' Agents.   Money Lenders.

Rooms 1 and 2, Knight Block,   TAMPA, FLA.

A word to visitors and probable investors whom we make it our business to meet. If you wish to invest in Tampa, or elsewhere in Florida, or if you want information concerning investments in Hillsborough, our native county, we claim to be able to furnish it accurately and in detail. You are respectfully invited to our office where you can see the only complete map of the city of Tampa, enlarged to 12x16 feet, oil painted. Also other maps and charts of interest. In accepting above invitation do not feel that you are expected to invest. It is our purpose that every new comer should get facts and figures and if possible a favorable impression of our State, county and city.

DR. SANFORD W. ALLEN,

DENTIST.

GOLD AND PORCELAIN CROWNS AND BRIDGES.

Cor. Franklin and Lafayette Sts.
Suites 1 and 3 Campbell Block.   TAMPA, FLA.

C. B. FITCH,

DEALER IN

Books, Stationery, School Supplies,

PERIODICALS JEWELRY, Etc.

TAMPA, - - - FLA.

hung on either side with costly tapestry and rare pictures, and lead past staircases of richly carved mahogany, at the foot of which on either side bronze pedestals support life-size Moorish figures, true to life in semi-barbaric costume, each holding aloft a cluster of electric lights whose terminal branches are crescents.

The walk down the hall from the office to the dining-saloon is perhaps the most remarkable panorama in the entire place. Certainly no other building in America holds anything like it. Other hotels have striking effects in the elegant parlors and dining-rooms, over which it is easy to be rapturous, but no other hotel, nor any other building outside the great exposition art gallery, has ever presented such an in-door promenade as this.

Visitors pass between two Japanese vases six feet high, clumps of growing palms in majolica tubs five feet in diameter. Reclining gnomes guard the portals of the grand parlors. On one side a terra-cotta half-relief picture of Spanish serenaders; on another, one of water carriers. Carved mahogany chairs of quaintest designs are sandwiched between onyx tables, on one of which stands a punch bowl with a scrap of German wassail song on its side; on another, a bowl of cut flowers, a graceful urn of finest bronze, or a quaint old clock of ebony and gold. Again, here is a grotesque Japanese figure, an elephant bearing a howdah of flowers on his back, a huge frog of majolica ware, an etching on the wall, a piece of priceless tapestry, a tempting tete-a-tete, or a mirror in antique frame.

And this is but a sample of the furnishings of the wondrous building. Yet the edifice pales into almost insignificance when compared with the grounds by which it is surrounded.

No words can adequately describe the beauty and luxury of this palace, which the Tampa people are proud of calling the eighth wonder of the world. It is one of the three celebrated Plant hotels, the Seminole at Winter Park,

Glimpses of Tampa.

W. H. Beckwith W. B. Henderson N. D. Smith G. C. Warren

The Beckwith-Henderson Co.,

Rooms 1, 2 and 3,
First National Bank and
Beckwith & Henderson Bld'g.

Real Estate

and Loans.

214 and 216 Franklin Street,

TAMPA, FLA.

Choice Business, Residence and Suburban Properties, also Orange Groves. Money Loaned at 8 and 10 per cent. net to Lender.

Reference: First National Bank, Tampa, or any Commercial Agency.

M. LOVENGREEN,
FURNITURE AND
UNDERTAKER
FRANKLIN ST., TAMPA, FLA.

and the Inn at Port Tampa, being the other two. All must be visited to be understood.

PLACES OF INTEREST NEAR TAMPA.

The Consumers' Electric Railway operates a perfect system of electric street and suburban railways. They have about twenty miles in service, and run their line with both a steam and water power-house. The steam plant is located in the city, but the dam and water power-house is about six miles from the city up the Hillsborough River, where they have a large head and a fall of about seventeen feet. They anticipate moving this plant down the river three miles, and expect to increase their power fully eighty per cent.

A ride over any part of the line is a pleasure, but the system affords places of special interest. Ballast Point lies down the bay about six miles, and is about a thirty minutes' ride from the bridge spanning the Hillsborough River. At the Point a splendid dancing pavilion, at the water's edge, affords much pleasure to frequent parties of young people from the city.

Palmetto Beach, or East Tampa, is a new suburb just in its infancy. It is here that one of the most attractive and complete cigar factories in this vicinity is located. Garcia Guerra's factory is said to be the most tasty in design of the structures of this order. Salvador Rodriguez has a large factory here also.

There is a natural park of much beauty at the terminus of the electric railway, and the building of a pavilion is contemplated.

The electric railway connects Tampa, West Tampa, Ybor City, East Tampa and Ballast Point, affording great convenience to visitors and residents.

Port Tampa and Picnic Island, located on the South Florida Railway about nine miles, are points that the visitor should not miss.

At Port Tampa the Plant Investment Company is

TAMPA
STAR ★ HOUSE.

HOUSE FURNISHING GOODS.
DRY GOODS and NOTIONS.

Earthenware, Lamps, Tin, Glass, Wood and Willow Ware, Fancy China, Novelties, Dolls, Toys, Games, Children's Wagons.

AGENTS FOR BUTTERICK'S PATTERNS.

Franklin Street, Next Door to Post Office,

TAMPA, - - - FLORIDA.

making marvelous improvements in the line of creating facilities for shipping; large berths have been dredged out electric elevators are being erected for loading phosphate, large quantities of which are shipped from this point.

It is here that the Inn, a hotel accommodating seventy-five, is built three-quarters of a mile from the shore. More desirable quarters could not be found.

The grounds of the Tampa Bay Hotel are under the care of a thorough gardener, and should by all means be visited. Here one will find the greatest profusion of the rarest kind of tropical and semi-tropical plants, flowers and trees. The hotel is worth a long journey to see, being one of the most elegantly furnished buildings in this country and probably unsurpassed in point of variety.

The "Garrison," where the old government post was located, is also of interest. It lies at the foot of Franklin street in the southern portion of the town.

The city is lighted by two electric light plants, and will soon have gas also.

A most efficient fire department and a water works system of the highest order keep the rate of insurance down.

Schools—In this county there are ninety white and thirteen colored schools, with 4,600 pupils.

In the city there are thirteen white and three colored schools, with about 2,000 pupils.

A children's home, where little unfortunates are cared for, is a most worthy institution.

An emergency hospital is another institution deserving much credit.

Both of these institutions owe their existence to the efforts of two boards of lady managers. Here, certainly, is an opportunity for some philanthropist to help worthy causes.

Parties wishing information can obtain all they desire from the following:

On Real Estate—Beckwith & Henderson, Hendry &

Knight, J. M. Fernandez, Salomonson & Fessenden, Hugh C. Macfarlane, H. J. Cooper.

On Trucking and Farming—The Neylan family at their place, east of Ybor City about half a mile.

On Orange Culture—W. R. Fuller, Beckwith & Henderson, Captain John T. Lesley.

On Phosphate—Thomas Palmer, T. M. Weir, Hendry & Knight.

On Cigar Industry and General Information—F. A. Salomonson, Gaoino Gutierrez, John T. Lesley, W. B. Henderson.

On Municipal Affairs—Perry G. Wall, W. H. Beckwith, John C. Jeffcott.

On County Affairs—C. E. Harrison, Charles Wright, W. E. Bledsoe.

On Boating, Sailing, Rowing, Fishing, etc.—Percy Culbreath, bridge keeper.

Tampa Bay Hotel, D. P. Hathaway, manager. Will accommodate 600 people. Rates $5.00 per day and up.

The Inn, Port Tampa, C. G. Logan, manager. Accommodations for 75. Rates $3.00 and $4.00 per day; $21.00 and $24.00 per week.

Almeria, Tampa, corner Franklin and Washington streets. Proprietor, H. T. Lykes. Will accommodate 75 to 100. Rates $2.50 to $4.00 per day; $15.00 to $17.00 per wek; $50.00 per month.

DeSoto Hotel. Proprietors, Lewis & Dunn. Corner Zack and Marion streets. Accommodates 100. Rates $2.50 to $3.50 per day; special by the week.

Palmetto Hotel, corner Florida avenue and Polk street. R. F. Webb, proprietor. Accommodates 100. Rates $2.00 to $3.00 per day; $8.00 to $12.00 per week.

Plant Hotel, corner Ashley and Madison streets. Proprietor, J. A. Roberts. Will accommodate 60. Rates $1.50 to $2.00 per day; $7.00 per week.

Crescent Hotel, Franklin street. Proprietor, Mrs. F.

B. Jones. Accommodates 200. Rates $2.00 to $2.50 per day; $10.00 per week; $30.00 per month.

City Hotel, Ashley street, near Southern Florida despot. Proprietor, W. A. McCord. Accommodates 40. Rates $1.50 to $2.00 per day; $7.00 per week; $25.00 per month.

Avenue Hotel, on Florida avenue, near Southern Florida depot. Accommodates 25, Proprietor, G. Van D. Elden. Rates $2.00 per day; special rates by week or month.

Collins House, Ashley and Whiting streets. Proprietor, A. B. Wheelock. Accommodates 25. Rates $1.50 per day; $6.00 per week; $25.00 per month.

Private Boarding Houses—Mrs. A. H. Carruthers, corner Twigg and Pierce streets. Rates $2.00 per day, $10.00 per week for one person; $18.00 for two.

Mrs. Carew, in the Garrison. Rates 7.00 per week; $30.00 per month for one; $50.00 for two.

Mrs. J. A. Loveless, Lafayette street. Rates $5.00 per week.

These hotels come in about the order of their importance, but here, as elsewhere, it is possible to rent furnished or unfurnished rooms. If unfurnished, all that is needed to put them in the most comfortable and elegant order may be procured at the house M. Lovengreen, on Franklin street. This is the oldest furniture house in Tampa, and the largest.

All kinds of earthenware, china, lamps, willow-ware and other house-furnishings and notions will be found at the Tampa Star House on the same street.

Stationery, all kinds of reading matter, periodicals, etc., will be found at the book store of C. B. Fitch also, on Franklin street. He has a full assortment.

Prominent Physicians—Dr. Jackson, Dr. Stebbins, Dr. W. E. Norton, Drs. Lawrence & Abernathy, Drs. Weedon & Bird, Drs. Petty & Mathews, Dr. Oppenheimer, Drs.

Douglass & Beard. Homeopathic Physicians—Drs. Stafford, Larner and Bruce.

Dentists—Dr. S. W. Allen, corner Franklin and La Fayette streets, in suites 1 and 3, in Campbell Block, does fine work.

Orlando.

Distance from Jacksonville 148 miles. Fare from Jacksonville $4.65. Take J., T. K. & W. at Union Depot.

Population in September, 1895, 4,000.

Orlando, the capital of Orange county, Florida, is a phenomenal city, situated in the banner county of the Orange Belt.

It is built on the culmination of the ridge or plateau of the peninsula, between the Atlantic ocean and the Gulf of Mexico; and it is a remarkable fact that the water falling within the city limits flows in opposite directions—the one into the Atlantic and the other into the Gulf of Mexico.

It is on the highest elevation in the county, being ninety-three feet above Sanford, only twenty-three miles distant.

The water supply is from a deep spring lake, conveyed by a magnificent system of water works, with a stand-pipe 125 feet high, with an average pressure of fifty pounds to the square inch, the direct pressure from the engines in case of fire being 150 pounds.

There is a well-organized fire company, with proper equipments for any emergency.

The sanitary arrangements are unique and efficacious. The health of the city testifies to the purity of the air and the water, the average deaths being ten to one thousand per year, notwithstanding the influx of many sick people and consumptives in the last stages of disease.

The county seat was established at Orlando in 1856, the

court house being built of rough pine logs. In 1873 there were but three stores and 150 inhabitants. It was then that the cowboys, of all ages, or crackers (so called from the skillful use of the long cowhide whip,) came in companies, taking the town by storm, with their whoops and yells, riding their ponies and carrying beneath them saddle-bags of Spanish gold, a pistol in one hand and a flask of whisky in the other.

The impetus of growth began in 1880, and there are now over one hundred two or three-story brick buildings.

The countryman may not now, as of yore, ride up to *the* store, calling for his bacon and grits, his hardware, dry goods, tobacco and mail, but must make a tour of the city for his purchases.

There are five dry goods stores, seven groceries, three shoe stores, a candy factory, a large hardware and queensware establishment, two grain stores and four bakeries, saying naught of the paint shops, furniture stores and innumerable shops and smaller establishments.

There is a good brick public school building, with an attendance of several hundred pupils, besides there are several private schools, a Catholic convent school and a flourishing kindergarten.

There are six handsome churches, and on the Sabbath the streets are deserted and the churches full, all the business houses being closed.

Orlando is accessible on all sides by railroad, and holds out to the tourist and home-seeker as much solid comfort, pleasure and enterprise as any city of its size in the South.

Leaving Jacksonville, either by way of Sanford or Ocala, the ride of six hours is a flitting panorama of flourishing towns and suburban residences, with their orange groves, picturesque windmills, truck gardens, apiaries and teeming poultry yards.

The traveler hardly finds himself in the country before he is in town again, so closely do the outskirts of one town

THE SAN JUAN,

Orlando, Florida.

WILLIAMS & BEEMAN,
Proprietors.

The Largest
and only Exclusive

TOURIST HOTEL

In Orlando.

First-Class Service.   +   Pleasant Rooms.

REASONABLE TERMS.

Rates $3.00 to $4.00 per day.
Special terms by week or month.

THE PINES,

ORLANDO, FLA.

MRS. OLIVER CARPENTER,
Proprietress.

RATES, $1.50 per Day; $8 to $10 per Week.

overlap those of another, with perhaps a bit of piney woods, a bay head or lake intervening, until the residences nestle more closely together, the smoke stacks and spires appear, and the conductor announces Orlando.

There are in and near Orlando thirteen lakes, fed by boiling springs and kept pure by brisk outlets; and ever and anon may be heard the merry laugh and frolic of her sons and daughters as they sport their light craft upon the waters.

The ice factory, water works, planing mills, fertilizer companies, wagon factories and other manufacturing establishments, serve to keep the revenue at home and give employment to many of her people.

There is a street car line running the length of the city, several well-kept livery stables, two national banks, a foundry, four hotels and numerous boarding houses. There are houses to rent, suites of rooms furnished and unfurnished, so that all may be suited in their domestic and culinary arrangements.

The rate of board is from $15.00 per month up to $2.00 and $3.00 per day.

There is the finest brick three-story market house in the State, with paved floors and marble slabs, kept, clean and sweet; and it is indeed a treat in midwinter, passing down the broad aisle, to see the fine meats, fresh and salt water fish, crisp vegetables and flowers that are offered for sale.

The housekeeper, filling her basket there, may pass on to the bakeries, and order everything from cooked meats, bread and hot rolls down to a lady finger, gathering up a dainty and substantial menu, after the daily visits of the milk and ice wagons.

People *live* in Orlando, and live *well*. They are a merry, happy people, dreading no long winters, never having experienced an epidemic, given to hospitality, always extending a cordial welcome to the stranger.

WM. B. JACKSON, Pres. C. R. SWITZER, Vice-Pres.
J. L. GILES, Cashier.

FIRST NATIONAL BANK

OF ORLANDO,

Transacts a General Banking Business.

N. Y. Correspondent: Hanover National Bank.
Jacksonville Correspondent: First National Bank of Florida.

OPEN ALL THE YEAR. UNDER NEW MANAGEMENT.

MAGNOLIA HOTEL,

ORLANDO, FLA.

RATES $2.00 AND $2.50 PER DAY.

MRS. HAZEL-MILES, P. W. HAZEL,
Proprietress. Manager.

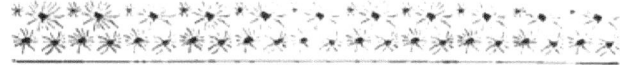

This is a city of organizations, churches, lodges, literary and social clubs, base ball and bicycle clubs.

There is a fine South Florida Fair building, with extensive grounds, a race track and a bicycle track.

The streets are paved with hard clay and the sidewalks are of cement.

Water oaks shade either side of the broad streets, and the well-dressed and well-kept people who walk up and down do not in any way suggest the *freeze*.

The orange trees are not dead! The people have more faith in them than ever, since it has been proven that they can stand a freeze. The sunshine and showers of one summer have wooed into luxuriant growth long, green sprouts that reach almost as high as the old growth, and it is confidently believed that next February, the anniversary of the freeze, will find the accustomed orange blossom instead of the icicle.

The people have lost two whole crops, and they have cheerfully retrenched on clothing and luxuries, but there has been more to eat, at a lower price, than ever before. The coming winter will find the bins and store-houses better filled with home produce than before the freeze, and herein we find a blessing in disguise. It has forced upon the people the lesson of home production. The winter gardens are being planted now; and when the Ice King holds the North in fetters, Orlando and other Florida towns will be shipping carloads of egg plant, tomatoes, cucumbers, new potatoes, peas, snap beans and strawberries. It is a daily sight now to see the streets swept by overflowing loads of sweet-scented hay, and many have been compelled to pull down their barns and build larger to receive their corn, rice, sugar, syrup, pumpkins, sweet potatoes and provender.

The loss of a year of the *golden orange* has taught the people to go to work and keep the *golden dollar* at home.

The Niagara grape and Japan persimmon culture have

been greatly benefited by the freeze, and there is no pleasanter manner of passing an afternoon than driving to the extensive Niagara grape vineyards and persimmon groves.

A delightful jaunt on the railroad is to Lake Charm, where the gentlemanly and enthusiastic florist, Mr. T. L. Mead, never tires of displaying his rare plants and magnificent grounds. He is making a specialty of orchids, crotons and palms.

Mr. Allen, of Pine Castle, four miles off on the South Florida Railroad, holds like inducements; and those who do not find his roses in bloom, will find at all seasons something rare and beautiful.

The homes in Orlando are luxurious, commodious and hospitable. Flowers are extensively cultivated, and the people live much of their time out of doors or on their porches, hammocks being in great requisition the year round.

There are within reach of Orlando many pleasure resorts. The Atlantic and Gulf coasts attract many for fishing and bathing. Clay Spring is a few hours' by carriage or railroad, and is a deep, clear boiling spring of sulphur water, forming a basin navigable for yachts and small steamboats, and it is thither the picnicers and strawriders ofttimes resort by sunlight or moonlight.

Fort Gatlin, with its fine lakes and trout fishing, its old oak trees and wind-tossed gray moss, attracts many to spend the day, with well-filled baskets to supplement the fish-fry.

Winter Park, two miles off by rail or carriage road, offers the literary and musical entertainments of Rollins College, to say naught of the ample facilities for yachting and horseback riding.

Orlando is prepared to suit the tastes of all with her schools, churches, hotels, opera house, banks, newspapers and social entertainments.

The leading hotel is the San Juan, kept by Williams & Beeman, two ambitious young men. One of them is a nephew of the veteran hotel man, Warren Leland, under whose instruction he has been taught to run a hotel. There is little doubt about the ability of his master, and none at all of the aptitude of the pupil. The San Juan will bear inspection and acquaintance. Rates $3.00 to $4.00 per day. Capacity 100.

Another hotel which opens this year under new management as an all-the-year-hotel is the Magnolia. Its rates are $2.00 to $2.50 per day. It is favorably situated, not far from the depot, and but two blocks from the court house.

A refined, genteel, home-like place, more like a pleasant private house than a hotel, is "The Pines," on Orange avenue, kept by Mrs. Olive Carpenter. Terms $1.50 per day or $8.00 per week.

Those wishing safe advisors on arriving in Orlando will find disinterested and candid as well as able advisors in Mr. Mahlon Gore, Mr. J. K. Duke, Curtis & O'Neal, Mr. Dixon and Mr. Sperry.

The best physicians are Dr. Porter, homeopathic, Drs. Persons & Harriss, partners in allopathy.

The most reliable law firm is Massey & Baumgarten.

Nicholson, the best curio dealer.

Mr. Gore is the most reliable real estate dealer.

Best livery stable proprietors, Mennefee & Palmer, opposite San Juan Hotel.

The best first-class hotel, San Juan.

The best first-class boarding-house, Mrs. Carpenter's.

The best druggists, Dr. McElroy and Mr. Lawrence.

The leading bank, the First National Bank of Orlando, W. B. Jackson, president.

Winter Park.

Distance from Jacksonville 144 miles. Fare $4.45. Take F. C. & P., or Plant System.

Winter Park is an incorporated town near the center

Rollins' College, Winter Park.

A View in Winter Park.

of Orange county, on the line of the Southern Division of the Plant Railroad System in Florida. Its site was selected by its first settlers with especial reference to its healthfulness and beauty as a residence town. In these important respects it has always been greatly appreciated by the many visitors who have returned season after season to its hotels, and by those who occupy its pleasant cottages, many of the latter remaining the whole or a greater part of the year.

In point of elevation Winter Park is among the higher places in Florida, well open to all the winds that blow and free from all unsanitary conditions. It has five good sized lakes withi nor partly within its borders, but the banks are bold, there are no swampy or unsightly margins, and the streams connecting the lakes have a swift current, so that the waters are always fresh and pure. The lakes, in fact, are a frequent resort for pleasure or fishing, and add a very important element to the beauty of the town.

It is not claimed for Winter Park that it is a business center, although it has four general stores, two apothecary stores, a stationery store, a bakery, livery stable, etc., but no saloon. It has two physicians of excellent repute, a good dentist and all necessary mechanics.

The leading hotel in Winter Park, the Seminole, is well known throughout the country as second to no other in Florida for beauty of location, excellence of management, and especially for its success in promoting a home-like contentment in all its guests, who have a habit of returning season after season to its spacious rooms and admirably served table. Almost the same things can be said of the Rogers House, except as to size. Both hotels command fine views of Lake Osceola, and are surrounded by pleasant grounds. The Seminole, however, is open only during the usual short season from January 1st to April 1st, while the Rogers House receives guests from October to June. Besides these there are two first-class boarding houses—that of Mr. D.

N. Bachelor, opposite the Seminole, and that of Mrs. Morton, in the "Pansy Cottage."

There are three religious societies in Winter Park—the Episcopalian, Congregationalist and Methodist, the latter two having settled ministers.

It is, however, the presence of Rollins College in Winter Park that bestows upon the town its greatest distinction. This institution is now ten years old, and in that time it has acquired a fine reputation for thorough work in all its departments. It maintains a preparatory school, as it is obliged to do for a time in this new country, and does so with great success, but its classical, scientific, musical and art departments are given greater prominence and have merited high commendation. The college has always attracted many students from the North and West, who find it desirable to escape from the inclemency of the colder parts of the country. Here they can pursue their studies under favorable conditions as to health and lose no time by the way. A fine, well-equipped gymnasium building secures good physical training, and lawn tennis, boating and ball playing are never interrupted by unfavorable weather. The college campus contains about twenty acres, and is situated on the highest land in town, overlooking Lake Virginia. The fees for tuition and the price for board at the college are very low, and these and all other particulars concerning the institution will be given on application to Prof. J. H. Ford, acting president.

The public schools—primary and grammar—are accommodated in a spacious and handsome building, said to be the best school-house in the county. The schools are taught by excellent, trained teachers, according to the most approved methods.

A pleasant reading-room is maintained by the ladies of the Christian Temperance Union, who own their building and keep the rooms supplied with current papers and magazines free to all.

Perhaps one of the best appreciated institutions in

Winter Park is the Free Public Library. It contains some ten hundred well-selected volumes, to which there are frequent additions. The college library is also opened to residents and visitors, and is well supplied with standard and reference books. These libraries taken together, and offered free to all, make it probable that no town of its size anywhere is better supplied with good literature than this of Winter Park.

A word may be said about the social life of the town. This is just what might be expected in a small community made up largely of cultivated people. The literary and musical elements are quite prominent. Lectures and concerts are quite frequent, those at the college being accessible to all. The Seminole parlors are open to those who enjoy dancing. In these ways and by the cordiality of family and friendly intercourse there are always maintained the pleasant amenities of a refined social life.

A year ago much would have been said of the extensive and well-grown orange groves. Their loss is deeply felt, but a few years will restore them, and in the meantime the cultivators of the soil are doing much in other directions.

There are many fine residences in and near Winter Park, occupied during the winter by well-known people from Northern and Western States. Among these may be mentioned Rev. Dr. Kedney, of Faribault, Minn.; Mr. F. W. Lyman, of Minneapolis, Minn.; Mr. Wm. C. Comstock, of Chicago, Ill.; Mr. James Ronan, of Trenton, N. J.; Prof. W. J. Kirkpatrick, of Philadelphia, Pa.; Mr. C. G. Zousey, of New York; Rev. Dr. Ripley, of Buffalo, N. Y.; Mr. Gilbert Hart, of Detroit, Mich.; Miss Sparrell, of Boston, Mass.; Mr. H. B. Crosby, of Paterson, N. J.; Mr. Geo. D. Rand, of Boston, Mass.; Mr. Chauncey Denny, of Northfield, Vt.; Mr. J. H. Wyeth, of St. Louis, Mo.; Mr. Charles E. Smith, of Boston, Mass.; Mr. Wm. Schultz, of

New Jersey, and Mr. Robert W. Given, of Philadelphia, Pa.

Orlando, the county seat, five miles south of Winter Park, is reached by rail over the Southern Division of the Savannah, Florida and Western Railroad, and also over the Oviedo Branch of the Florida Central and Peninsular Railroad. Going east, Oviedo and Lake Charm are reached through Gabriella and Goldenrod. The drives about the country under the pine trees, along the lakes and among the orange groves are always pleasant, but will be still pleasanter when the roads are clayed or shelled, as the most important of them must be at no distant day.

The streets and sidewalks of Winter Park are perhaps better taken care of than those of most other Florida towns. This is partly owing to the fact that the town government takes a proper pride in their good condition and in the care of the public parks in the center of the town, and partly to the enthusiastic and effective work of the Village Improvement Society, which has set out shrubbery and hundreds of shade trees, supplementing the work of the town and creating a fine public sentiment in favor of well-kept grounds and streets.

Taken altogether, the people of Winter Park are quite justified in quoting the enthusiastic exclamation of President Arthur at the time of his visit in 1883, the town being then only in the third year of its settlement: "This," said he, " is the prettiest spot I have seen in Florida."

For information as to real estate, cottages to rent, board, etc., apply to Mr. H. S. Chubb or to Mr. Chas. J. Ladd.

Lake City.

Distance from Jacksonville 60 miles. Fare $2.40. Take the F. C. & P. R'y at Union Depot.

This is a town of about 2,100 inhabitants. It was originally an Indian trading post, and bore the name of

West End of Barracks—Florida Agricultural College.

A Company of Volunteers—Florida State Agricultural College.

Lancaster, in honor of Judge Lancaster, one of the conspicuous characters of early days. It afterwards became the county seat for three counties, Bradford, Baker and Suwannee, and changed its name to Alligator. In a few years some of its inhabitants objected, when away from home, to being introduced as "Alligator, ladies and gentlemen," and the name was again changed to Lake City. Later, when the counties were differently laid out, Columbia county was carved from surplus territory, and Lake City became its county seat.

It is one of the prettiest and most prosperous places in the State. It is almost surrounded by a series of charming lakelets, which give a most pleasing effect to the landscape, and are large enough to afford, besides unlimited fishing, very pleasant sport in the way of sailing and rowing. Near by are located valuable phosphate mines. This is the junction of the Georgia Southern and Florida Railroad, from Macon, Ga. White Sulphur Springs is but a few miles from this station.

The principal attraction and most important feature of Lake City is the Florida Agricultural College and Government Experimental Station, which was removed to this place in 1884. This is a fine institution, located about three-quarters of a mile south of the city. It is supported mainly by the government, although the State has made some appropriations. It offers a full college curriculum, has a faculty of eighteen able professors, and has recently opened its doors to both sexes.

In addition to the usual classical and scientific courses, it gives instructions in scientific and practical agriculture, and in mechanic arts, practical working in woods and metals. A farm connected with the college gives opportunity for practical instruction in agriculture.

Two other experimental stations, one at DeFuniak, in West Florida, and one at Fort Myers, in South Florida, are under the charge of this central station. This institution is the pride of Lake City, and, indeed, of the State.

The hotels of Lake City are few and small. The Central and The Inn are the principal.

Mr. J. Potsdamer has a livery stable, and furnishes turnouts and drivers at reasonable rates. He meets all trains with carriages.

Dr. Appell and Dr. Chalker are able, up-to-date physicians. At Hunter's drug store may be found all that an invalid can need.

The country around abounds in quail and other small game.

Live Oak.

Distance from Jacksonville 82 miles. Fare from Jacksonville $3.25. Take F. C. & R'y at Union Depot.

This is a pleasant little town; important because it is the gateway into the State from the west. It is at this point that the Savannah, Florida and Western Railroad, of the Plant System, enters the State. Passengers from Cincinnati, Louisville and the West may, by this route, penetrate directly to the center or western portion of the peninsula without the detour to Jacksonville as a starting point.

Live Oak is just now enjoying a pleasant impulse to her prosperity in an extensive saw mill, recently erected by Dowling & Co., and which is turning out large quantities of lumber. An ice factory has also been erected within the past few months, and is doing a fine business.

Six miles from Live Oak, on the Savannah, Florida and Western Road, is situated the Lower Suwannee Springs, a most picturesque place, where are numerous springs noted for their medicinal qualities. A company of capitalists from Savannah has recently purchased the entire property, and have put it in fine condition.

The Ethel House is the principal hotel of Live Oak, and is situated across the street from the depot.

Tallahassee.

Distance from Jacksonville 165 miles. Fare from Jacksonville $6.60. Take the F. C. & P. R'y at Union Depot.

This is the State capital, and is a gas-lighted city, with street cars and water works. It is on the Florida Central and Peninsular Railroad, 165 miles west of Jacksonville, and about 200 east of Pensacola. Its site was selected in 1824 as the capital of the then newly-acquired territory, not because of commercial facilities (for there were no railroads in those days), but by reason of its central position in the then sparsely-settled country, its nearness to the Gulf of Mexico, and especially because of the rich lands of the surrounding country that would attract settlers. After the cession of the Floridas to the United States, and Congress had passed an act organizing the Territory, the President appointed Wm. P. Duval Governor, and "a council of thirteen of the most fit and decent persons of the Territory," in accordance with said act. Previous to these times Gen. Andrew Jackson, by virtue of his office as Commandant, had acted as Governor. Governor Duval, though, was the first civil Governor. The first session of the Territorial Council was held in the city of Pensacola, the capital of West Florida, in September, 1822; the second session in St. Augustine, the capital of East Florida, in June, 1823. As the two capitals were about 400 miles apart, it was thought better to select a more central position. Accordingly, at the session aforesaid it was ordered that the Governor appoint a commission, who should carefully examine the topography and resources of some central location, and after the commission should make their report the Governor was to issue his proclamation, calling a meeting of the legislative council at that point. The commission selected the present site in July, 1824. Governor Duval issued his proclamation from St. Marks, requiring the legislative council to assemble on or about the 21st of December, 1824, "at a point one-half mile southwest of the Tallahassee old fields, where it intersected the Ochlochnee Trail, in the county of Gadsden." Here the thirteen solons of the new Territory assembled in due time in the "capitol building," which consisted of a hastily constructed log hut, and was located in the southeast corner of what is now the Capitol Square. One of their first acts was to incorporate and lay off the town of Tallahassee, which embraced only 160 acres, or one-quarter of a mile square. This act was approved by the Governor on the 24th of December, 1824. Subsequently at the same session an act was passed organizing the new county of Leon, and Tallahassee was made the county site.

The location of the seat of government at this point showed the wisdom of the selectors. The lands of the surrounding country were of unparalleled fertility, while the absence of swamps and marshes incident to a flat country, was a sure token that no deadly malaria prevailed. Soon settlers flocked here from all parts of the Union—so much so that the desert rejoiced and blossomed as the rose, and in less than a couple of decades there was more wealth, culture and refinement, and a greater population than in any other section of Florida. Here visitors were entertained with lavish hospitality, and guests coming from other States were astonished at the ease, elegance, and refinement of the society of that day. Minds cultivated by travel in European lands and stored with knowledge from well-selected libraries, coupled with wealth, gave a state of society second to no place in the United States. Nor was this all. There was a spirit of enterprise and progressness among these people of the old territorial days. A bank (the Central) was soon established, and in the early thirties a railroad to St. Marks was projected. This road was commenced in 1835 and completed in 1837 to its Gulf terminus, a distance of twenty-two miles, so that Tallahassee justly claims to have constructed the third railroad in the United States. Cotton, which was then the great

J. T. BERNARD, Attorney-at-Law, | O. BERNARD, Civil Engineer,
Resident of Florida 42 Years. | Native Floridian.

J. T. BERNARD & SON,

REAL ESTATE

Insurance and Financial Agents,

TALLAHASSEE, FLA.

Land Sold, Purchased, Surveyed, Inspected and Mapped.
Town Sites Laid Out. Legal Business Promptly Attended To.

ST. JAMES HOTEL,

TALLAHASSEE, FLA.

Open all the Year.

First-Class in Every Respect.

SITUATED IN THE VERY CENTRE OF THE TOWN.

ACCOMMODATES 75 TO 100.

RATES:

$2 to $2.50 per Day; $10 to $12.50 per Week.

G. A. LAMB, Proprietor.

staple product, was brought here from all the surrounding country, even from a number of counties in Georgia, while regular lines of vessels plied between St. Marks and New York and New Orleans. But her energetic citizens were not satisfied with a Gulf outlet. After railroads were being constructed in Georgia and the sections of country that formerly sent its produce to Tallahassee was reached by a railroad from Savannah, Tallahassee determined to have an Atlantic as well as a Gulf outlet. Accordingly its leading citizens succeeded in getting through the Legislature the celebrated Internal Improvement act of 1855, which not only enabled them to connect with Jacksonville and Fernandina on the east, and with Pensacola on the west, but has contributed more than any other act to develop the resources of the entire State. So to Tallahassee is our State indebted for the numerous railroads that traverse her surface. Under this act the P. & G. R. R. (now a part of the F. C. & P. system) was built in 1857-8 from Tallahassee to Lake City, where it connected with the Central to Jacksonville. Subsequently it was extended to the Apalachicola River, where it now connects with the railroad to Pensacola.

Tallahassee has been truly called the Garden City. Beautiful for situation, the joy of its people, it is a floral home to its designers, for there is not a house but which is embowered with flowers of various hues and varieties. These beauties of nature thrive here to perfection, and such is the reputation of this section in that respect that it often happens that orders are received from distant points. What an opening for a florist! The good people here do not raise for market, but gladly *give away* all they can spare. Situated on the crests of lofty hills, the view of the surrounding country is entrancing. The elevation is about 200 feet above sea level. From the observatory on the capitol, court house or St. James Hotel, on a clear day, may sometimes be seen the smoke from the so-called "volcano" in Jefferson county, forty miles to the southeast.

This volcano is a mystery. There are those, intelligent persons, too, who thoroughly believe in its existence. For a century past, both during the Spanish reign as well as our own, fishermen have seen at night a bright light, and during the day a dense cloud of smoke. Detonations, too, have been heard at different places, but the direction of the sound radiating from the same point proves that it is where the smoke comes from. Repeated efforts have been made to solve this mystery, but an impenetrable morass bars progress. A party once succeeded in approaching within a few miles. By nailing cleats he succeeded in climbing a high tree, and from his position he saw a few miles distant a plateau, from the center of which a dense smoke ascends. The New York *Herald* and one or two other publications have offered liberal rewards to solve the mystery, but notwithstanding the Florida volcano still remains either a myth or a reality.

The rides and scenery in this section are delightful; no sandy roads, but good hard clay, so that one can spin along at a rapid rate. Hill and dale, sparkling streams and lakes abound. Such a scene of picturesque beauty is well worth a visit.

In the cemetery here are buried Prince Achille Murat and his wife, who was a grandniece of General Washington. The Prince lived at Fernandina in 1820, subsequently removed to this section where he married. Old settlers state that the late Emperor Napoleon III. was a guest of his cousin, the Prince, for a year, and was known as Captain Bonaparte. Prince Murat died in 1845 and his widow in 1857.

A favorite resort for visitors and picnic parties is the celebrated Wakulla Spring, the head of Wakulla River. It is sixteen miles south of Tallahassee, and is said to be a greater natural curiosity than Silver Spring in Marion county, near Ocala. The Wakulla Spring has a depth of 190 feet, and so clear is the water that a silver 5-cent piece can be easily seen at the bottom. Boats are there to take visitors out; and on a clear day, as one looks into its transparent depths he almost feels as if he were suspended in the air, and a dizziness comes over him. A favorite amusement with visitors is to cast circular pieces of tin, and as they go down into the depths beneath all the prismatic colors are beautifully reflected.

A favorite drive in the vicinity of Tallahassee is to Live Oak, about two and a half miles north. This was the residence in former years of Hon. John Branch, Secretary of the Navy during a part of Jackson's administration, and the last of the Territorial Governors. Some years since it was purchased by a Scottish gentleman, Mr. E. H. Ronalds, now deceased, who spent thousands in beautifying it. Though the old mansion was destroyed by fire last year, it is still a beautiful place. The large spring at the foot of a hill which, through a hydraulic ram, supplies water for bathing and household purposes, the serpentine paths, the fountains, the well-kept lawn and beautiful groves—all conspire to make it an object of interest to the lover of the beautiful and picturesque.

Five miles northeast of Tallahassee is Ivanhoe, an estate belonging to another Scottish family. It borders on Lake Hall, a beautiful sheet of water. From the rear of the mansion a scene of wierd beauty presents itself—so much so that it is a favorite resort of tourists, many of whom, not satisfied with the view, photograph it, that they may have an interesting souvenir.

So beautiful are the views around Tallahassee, so delightful the drives, and so balmy the air, that visitors who have once been there never fail to repeat their visit. To the sportsman the country around is a paradise, for quail abound; while to those who are fond of piscatorial sports the lakes have plenty of fish. Lakes Jackson, Iamonia and Micossukie are from five to ten miles long and from a half to four miles wide. Besides these there are a number of smaller lakes abounding in fish. If the sportsman prefers a deer hunt, he can be gratified by going some ten or fifteen miles south of Tallahassee.

Lands are cheap and quite fertile, and can be purchased at from $3.00 to $25.00 per acre, according to location and the nature of the improvements and distance from Tallahassee.

Leon county is noted for its fine grades of Jersey and Alderney cattle, which are eagerly sought for by purchasers from East and South Florida. During the year 1894, 50,000 pounds of butter were shipped from this point to various places in East and South Florida. Mr. M. H. Johnson has a creamery five miles west of Tallahassee, and so great is the demand for his cheese that he cannot keep up the supply.

Should the visitor wish to enjoy the Gulf breeze, salt water bathing and aquatic sports, he has only to take the Carrabelle, Tallahassee and Gulf Railroad forty miles to Lanark, which lies on the Gulf. Here he will find a large and commodious hotel, lighted with gas, and each room connected with the office by electric bells. Bath houses and boats are for the use of the guests, and those who are fond of aquatic sports can be gratified.

There are two banks in Tallahassee—the First National and the Capital City; one large furniture store (W. D. Hart's) which carries the heaviest stock in this section; one opera house, and five white churches, to-wit: Roman Catholic, Episcopal, Presbyterian, Methodist and Baptist. The State Seminary west of the Suwannee is located here. This is officered by a fine corps of teachers, with a college curriculum, physiosophical and chemical apparatus and an endowment of about $5,000 a year. In consequence of this endowment rates of tuition are only nominal. A fine brick building, costing about $6,000, is devoted to the public schools. All these are for the whites. The negro, however, is not neglected. By their own efforts, assisted by the whites, they have their own churches and schools. They have five of the former, one Episcopal, two Methodist and two Baptist. Their academy is a fine building, with modern school furniture, is officered by seven teachers, all colored. Just outside of Tallahassee in the south, on a lofty hill, are the buildings of the State Colored Normal and Industrial College. This institution is presided over by Prof. Tucker, of Sierra Leone, Africa. He is doing a noble work for his race and for the State. The grounds, building, machinery, etc., are worth $75,000 or $100,000, and the institution is supported by the State and the United States. Many visitors go there and express both surprise and gratification.

At this time there is but one real estate agency, that of J. T. Bernard & Son, the former a resident of the State for forty-five years, and the latter a native. The son is a surveyor, and from his intimate knowledge of localities can give the prospector all needed information. This is a reliable firm.

One of the attractions of Tallahassee is its parks—not large ones, as in some of our large cities, but small ones, with their fountains and flowers. On McCarthy street, which is 200 feet wide, there are four, two of which have fountains and a fifth will soon be commenced.

Nor must we forget the University Library, Tallahassee's chief pride. Ten years ago a library association was formed. Ladies were appointed to solicit subscriptions. Now the association has 5,000 or more volumes on the shelves. On the walls in the hall are portraits of the first Territorial delegate to Congress, General Joseph M. Hernandez, Prince Achille Murat, and Governors Mosely, Brown, Walker and Perry. There is also a helmet and visor, supposed to have belonged to one of DeSoto's men. It was found in Jefferson county nearly fifty years ago. The library was initiated by the late ex-Governor D. S. Walker. He erected a two-story brick building, and deeded the upper portion to the trustees for the use of the library. Recently the trustees have received a gift of real and personal property valued at $5,000.

The United States Circuit Court House and Postoffice building is an imposing structure, costing $75,000. It is quite an ornament to the city.

There are two hotels, the Leon and St. James. Rates from $2.50 to $4.00 per day. Boarding houses charge from $30.00 to $50.00 per month.

The leading physicians are Dr. George Betton, Dr. Guinn and Dr. Philbrick.

Lanark-by-the-Sea.

A new railroad has lately been completed from Tallahassee to the Gulf coast, and terminating at Carrabelle, near the mouth of the Apalachicola River. Many pleasant little towns have sprung up along the route, and it has opened an extensive timber region. Along the coast of the Gulf of Mexico, thus made accessible, there are many points that are ideal summer resorts. These are coming to be known, and many are availing themselves of their delights.

One of these has a history, and that is Lanark-by-the-sea. Although for many years Mr. Clarke, of O. N. T. spool-cotton fame, has obtained his cotton from Florida, he never visited the State until 1894. He was so delighted with what he found that he at once invested in land. The point that pleased his fancy was a bay with a Venice-like curve on the Gulf coast, but protected from the outer winds and waves by a distant, long, low-lying island. Here, on rising ground that slopes to the sea, he has already erected a fine hotel elegantly furnished with all modern improvements; a long wharf; a large pavilion built almost over the water; bath houses, and every conceivable arrangement for the comfort and pleasure of himself, his friends, and all other guests. With loving loyalty, it has been named after Mr. Clarke's own town in Scotland—Lanark.

Panacea Springs.

Another of these summer resorts, much beloved by the favored few who know of its existence, is Panacea Springs. For this place take at Tallahassee the same Tallahassee and Carrabelle Railroad to a little station called Ashmore. Here, in summer, on Tuesdays, Thursdays and Saturdays, a hack meets the train and conveys passengers through the woods, a distance of six miles, to the springs. Here is a comfortable hotel, open all the year round and known as the Panacea Springs Hotel, with a capacity for twenty or twenty-five guests; terms, $1.00 per day, or $5.00 per week. Proprietor, G. F. Anderson.

The attractions at this place are fine sea-bathing, that may be indulged in every week in the year; the beach is fine, and, as is common along this shore, is shut in from the open Gulf by a distant island. The water is shallow and abounding in fish and oysters. Back of this place, within easy walking distance, are ponds or lakelets, where, in summer, wild ducks are plentiful; also, a variety of dark-colored wild geese, known locally as negro geese, make it a favorite haunt. These are small but edible, and huntsmen call shooting them capital sport.

In winter the wild ducks and all varieties of wild geese multiply upon the face of the water, and appear in immense quantities.

Quincy.

Distance from Jacksonville, 189 miles; fare from Jacksonville, $7.10. Take Florida Central and Peninsular Railway from Union Depot.

This beautiful little town is about twenty-five miles west of Tallahassee, and, like that city, lies among the red clay hills of Middle Florida. In traveling westward the marked change in the appearance of the country is surprising and grateful. The level sand of the pine woods, the

OWL CIGAR CO.,

NEW YORK AND FLORIDA.

MANUFACTURERS OF

FINE CIGARS.

New York Office, 204 East 27th Street.

Plantations and Factories, QUINCY, FLORIDA.

Manufacturers of the celebrated brands **ROBERT BURNS, ROYAL OWL, WHITE OWL, BELLE OF SARATOGA, CAPADURA**, and other well-known brands.

LOVE HOUSE,

QUINCY, FLORIDA.

Mrs. S. W. LOVE, - - Proprietress.

☞ Special Rates by Week or Month.

Free Sample Rooms.

wet swamps of the low hammocks, the sluggish water courses and quiet lakes, give place to high hills of red clay, firm and hard, groves of hickory, maple, wild cherry and other hard woods, singing brooks dancing down sloping hillsides.

Amid such a country as this nestles the pretty town of Quincy, just now possibly the most lively, wide awake town in Florida.

It was, until a few years ago, a typical old *ante-bellum* town, peopled by old, aristocratic, exclusive families, whose former slaves, in many instances, remained in their service, knowing but little difference, except that they received wages in place of the care, shelter and raiment of the olden times.

But little business, apart from the limited local trade, was transacted here. The rich soil, the kindly climate, the great variety of productions, and the cheapness of land, enabled every householder to be almost self-sustaining, and but little ambition was felt to be more.

But a change has come over the spirit of her dreams. Her streets hum with music of traffic and the bustle of trade. If one would see the transformation let him try to elbow his way through the densely crowded sidewalks on Saturday nights.

The principal cause of this is the revival of a half-forgotten industry. Tobacco was grown in this section in *ante-bellum* days, but only in the last few years has this industry been revived. At the instigation of Mr. H. R. Duval, president of the Florida Central and Peninsular Railroad Company, a number of New York capitalists, headed by Mr. George Storm, of the Owl Cigar Manufacturing Company, bought up thousands of acres, at a cost of several hundred thousands of dollars, and revived this most profitable industry, the success of which has been phenomenal.

The Owl Cigar Company, of New York and Florida, commenced their extensive operations in Gadsden county in the year 1887.

Views in Winter Park.

Residence of Geo. D. Rand, Esq., Winter Park, Fla.

This company owns 15,000 acres of the best farming land in Gadsden county, and they have invested over $300,000.00 in lands, together with the improvements on the same. They raise annually about 1,000 acres of tobacco. The output at the Quincy factory would represent 8,000,000 cigars per annum. On the plantations they have erected 142 tobacco barns of the most approved pattern. They have upward of 150 dwelling houses for the plantation employes, in addition to the superintendent's dwellings, stables, cattle sheds, etc. They operate eight large plantations, and, in addition to their tobacco crop, cultivate about 2,000 acres of land each year in corn, oats, sugar-cane, rice, potatoes, peas, etc.

Their headquarters are in the town of Quincy, where they have two large cigar factories; one is a brick building 125 by 124 feet, the other a two-story frame building 90 by 100 feet. In addition to these buildings, they have two large warehouses, one an extensive two-story building 60 by 80 feet in size, and the other a brick building of the same dimensions.

Some three years ago an artesian well was sunk on their factory lot, and this well furnishes an abundance of the finest water in the South. The Owl Cigar Company are now supplying water to the town of Quincy, by a special arrangement made with the Quincy Water Works Company.

The Owl Cigar Company have also discovered extensive mines of Fuller's earth on their plantations, and they have erected a large mill, which is fitted up with the most complete machinery. They grind and prepare the clay for market, and several varieties are shipped each week from the Quincy depot.

The company is keenly alive to the opportunities that exist in Florida, and have attracted a large colony of work people, who reside in the town of Quincy and its suburbs.

The country around produces all cereals but wheat,

and all fruits of the Western and Middle States—peaches, pears, grapes—and all the smaller fruits and berries.

Great quantities of sea-island and upland cotton are raised in this county. Sugar-cane is very extensively grown in this vicinity. From this little town of 1,500 inhabitants 5,000 barrels of syrup are shipped yearly as the surplus, or product over the demands of the home market.

In the centre of the town, which has grown up around it, is the house of the venerable Judge White. It is a genuine, typical *ante-bellum* planter's home—a large, roomy house of three stories, with wide, high portico, supported on immense round, fluted pillars, an overhanging balcony, wide hall running through the centre of the house, wide doors and large parlors. It is surrounded by ancestral oaks that shade extensive grounds. A hedge of Cherokee roses, running in wild riot over fence and tree and shrub, encloses the whole. A circular carriage road leads to the hospitable-looking front portico.

In sharp contrast are the elegant modern residences of Hon. R. H. M. Davidson, Hon. W. H. Davidson, W. M. Corry and others.

There are no prominent real estate firms in this town. The country is well settled up with a contented people, who do not care to sell their houses or lands.

Two livery stables do a thriving business—W. C. Wilson and Brackin & Co.

The most prominent physicians are Dr. Monroe, Dr. Scott, Dr. La Mar and Dr. Phillips of the allopathic school, and Dr. Kennedy, a successful homeopathist.

The principal hotel is the Love House, kept by Mrs. S. W. Love. It is a house of old and well sustained reputation, known all along the road to travelers of all degrees. Rates, $2.00 to $2.50 per day.

Another, recently opened, is the New Quincy, kept by Mrs. S. F. Cox. Rates, $2.00 per day; $7.00 per week.

Fernandina.

Distance from Jacksonville 30 miles. Fare from Jacksonville $1.50. Take F. C. & P. at Union Depot.

Fernandina has the largest and deepest harbor on the the eastern coast of the State. It is beautifully located in a sheltered situation on the west side of Amelia Island, the northern extremity of which guards the entrance to Cumberland Sound and the extensive land-locked harbor, into which open the St. Mary's River and Amelia River from Nassau inlet.

The city can well be proud of its harbor, it being the principal Atlantic terminus of the Florida Central and Peninsular Railroad Company, where it has one mile of docks and fine phosphate elevator and fertilizer depots, etc.

The city has nine lumber shipping firms; is the great shipping port for the large phosphate companies; also for cotton, naval stores, fruit and vegetables. It has two oyster canneries; a $100,000 lumber creosoting plant; one $150,000 palmetto fiber company; four saw and planing mills; a large ice factory; a number of cigar manufactories; a proprietary medicine factory, and the finest water works in the country. It has electric lights, broad, shady and well-paved streets. The situation is high, dry and healthy, with the Atlantic ocean on the east and the bay on the west. There are churches of all creeds, a public library, etc.

One of the chief attractions of Fernandina is the Amelia Beach, extending a distance of over twenty miles. The surface of the sand at the edge of the water is as hard as a floor, forming a magnificent drive, and a firm, hard shell road extends from the city to the beach, a distance of nearly two miles.

Connection is made at Fernandina semi-weekly with the elegant steamships of the Mallory line to and from New York; with Sea Island Route steamers to and from Savannah, and daily with Cumberland Route to and from

Brunswick, Macon, Atlanta, Chattanooga and all points West and Northwest.

A branch track from the city to the beach has been completed, and trains during the season run every hour to the seashore.

Eight miles from Fernandina, by water, on Cumberland Island, is the famous estate of Dungeness, bestowed by the State of Georgia upon General Nathaniel Greene, and belonging for many years to his descendants. Broad avenues, bounded by plantations of ancient orange and olive trees and lined with giant oaks, stretch grandly away on either side of the homestead. The old family burying-ground, with its ancient tombs (one of which covers the mortal part of the renowned soldier known to fame and the history of his country as "Light-Horse Harry" Lee) is located in a grove not far from the mansion.

Key West.

Distance from Jacksonville 480 miles. Fare from Jacksonville $18.40. Take Plant Line steamers from Port Tampa.

Key West, the county seat of Monroe county, is situated on an island, sixty miles from the nearest point on the mainland of Florida, and only ninety miles from Havana, Cuba. The island embraces two thousand acres of coral formation. The city has a population of 25,000, and is one of the most important naval stations in the United States. The custom house, the building for which cost over $100,000, is second in importance in the South, and transacts a revenue business of $11,000,000 per annum, requiring the services of fifty employes. The island contains sixteen square miles, and has eight miles of street railroad. It has gas and electric lights, a modern system of water works, a fine city hall and market, costing $80,000, and all the conveniences of a modern city, including live newspapers.

The cigar industry, although somewhat crippled within the last two years, is immense, there being at the time of this writing over 150 factories in operation in the city, giving employment to thousands of Cubans and Americans, and doing a business of $3,000,000 per annum. The sponge industry alone gives employment to a large number of men. The island presents many pleasing features to the tourist, and is well worth a visit; tropical trees and flowers of all kinds abound, and the people of the island are remarkably hospitable. A constant breeze from the Atlantic Ocean and the proximity of the Gulf Stream render the climate equable and delightful. Frost never reaches here. During the winter of 1895, when the northern and middle portions of the peninsula of Florida suffered from the frost, the lowest temperature at Key West was 54 degrees. Such a thing as artificial heat is unknown here, except for cooking purposes. The capacious wharves of the city are daily lined with vessels of every nation, and the commodities of the world find an exchange here. The importance of Key West, as one of the greatest commercial centers of the country, is assured by its geographical position, and with the completion of the Nicaragua Canal it will occupy a still more prominent position in the commercial world.

Madison, Florida.

Distance from Jacksonville, 110 miles; fare from Jacksonville, $4.35.

The town of Madison, which is the county seat of the county of Madison, is located upon the Florida Central and Peninsular Railroad, fifty-five miles east of Tallahassee, the capital of the State. It has about 900 population, thirty general stores, one weekly newspaper, a sixty-five-room hotel, several private boarding-houses, two grist mills, one of the finest systems of water works in the State, a well equipped volunteer fire department, four churches, and a good school that is operated at the public expense eight months in the year. Just beyond the city limits of the town is situated the plant of the Florida Manufacturing Company, which is the largest sea-island cotton ginnery in the world. It furnishes employment to near 100 operatives day and night, for six months in the year, and half as many for the remainder of the time.

Madison is the trading centre of the counties of Madison, Taylor and Lafayette, and the principal market in the State for the preparation of sea-island cotton for market. The Florida Manufacturing Company prepare large quantities of it for manufacture into thread by the famous Coats Thread Company. Taylor and Lafayette counties lay to the south of the first named and border the Gulf of Mexico, the contiguity of which tempers the weather both winter and summer: making the climate a most equable one. Never too hot nor too cold for any kind of work to be performed at any season. Madison county has high hills, and valleys, and her soil contains a good proportion of clay. All are splendid for farming, gardening and fruit growing, if reasonable allowance is made for the varieties of fruits specially adapted to each. In Madison pears, peaches and plums do well, and the orange can be grown, but is not to any extent. Here the pecan nut grows to perfection. Mr. B. F. Moseley, of Madison, has received an annual return from his grove of $12.00 to $15.00 a tree. Peaches grow to perfection. This county is yet "in the woods," and thousands of acres of land can be had almost for a song. Through this portion of the State is the finest general farming belt in the South, producing the finest staples of both varieties of cotton, small grains to perfection, vegetables in plenty and at all seasons.

Many of the lands in Madison county are fertile, and improved to such an extent that but little improvement will be necessary to make them as desirable as any one could wish in a country home. They are near schools and churches, so that these privileges may be enjoyed by all; are not too far from the railroad as to make travel or shipment thereby inconvenient, and the country is inhabited by a whole-souled, genial and hospitable people, who will always welcome the industrious home-seeker, and exercise those civil amenities that make intercourse with them pleasant, agreeable and desirable.

Madison county lies between the far-famed Suwannee on the east and the Aucilla on the west, is bountifully watered by clear, running streams and fresh water lakes, all of which teem with the finest fish. The woods, fields and swamp lands abound in such game as deer, turkey, squirrel, quail, etc. While the Gulf is in easy riding distance, and readily yields its abundance of fish to a little labor. Fine sulphur springs are also near.

Any further information regarding farm lands, wild lands, phosphate lands, business or residence lots in or near town, or in any other class of real estate, may be obtained by writing to Mr. A. H. West, of Madison.

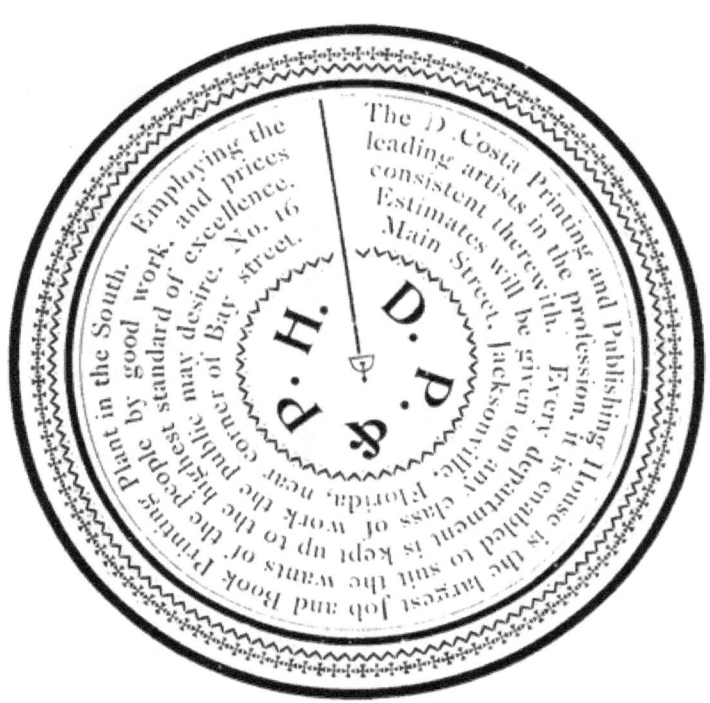

SILVER SOUVENIR
OF FLORIDA.
European Novelties.
BRIC-A-BRAC. CHOICE CHINA.

OLD SPANISH COAT OF ARMS.

Greenleaf & Crosby,
Jacksonville,
25 East Bay St.

ST. AUGUSTINE. PALM BEACH.
ALCAZAR, OPP. PONCE DE LEON. IN THE ROYAL POINCIANA.

www.ingramcontent.com/pod-product-compliance
Lightning Source LLC
Chambersburg PA
CBHW032230230426
43666CB00033B/1659